LOST
LAFAYETTE
COLORADO

LOST
LAFAYETTE
COLORADO

DOUG CONARROE

THE
History
PRESS

Published by The History Press
Charleston, SC
www.historypress.com

Front cover: author's collection.
Back cover: courtesy of Lafayette Public Library.

First published 2021

Manufactured in the United States

ISBN 9781467148238

Library of Congress Control Number: 2020945781

Notice: The information in this book is true and complete to the best of our knowledge. It is offered without guarantee on the part of the author or The History Press. The author and The History Press disclaim all liability in connection with the use of this book.

CONTENTS

INTRODUCTION

Lafayette, Colorado, was founded in 1888 by Mary E. Miller (1843–1921), who named the platted thirty-seven-acre town after her late husband. In a nutshell, the town is named after DeLafayette "Lafe" Miller (1840–1878), not the Marquis de Lafayette.

But wait. There's more.

In early 1861, Reverend Bennett Roberts, a minister from the Independence, Iowa Congregational Church, told his friends and parishioners about his exciting 1860 travels into the western end of Kansas Territory, where gold and silver miners in the foothills above Denver City could file a mining claim and strike it rich.

Until that chance encounter, the minister's neighbors and fellow Congregationalists Dr. John and Mary A. Miller and their tenant, George Henry Church, had no clue of the impact that Roberts's tale of traveling the Great American Desert would have on their families.

On April 24, 1861, native New Yorker George H. Church married Sarah Henderson Miller, daughter of John and Mary A. Miller and sister of DeLafayette Miller, who preferred to be called by his nickname, "Lafe." One month later, George and Sarah headed off for a mining claim near Idaho Springs in the newly formed Colorado Territory with two hitched teams of oxen pulling their wagon.

It took just a few months for George to abandon dreams of striking it rich in the remote mountainous region. He sold his claims and purchased land near Mount Vernon Canyon in Jefferson County, then later settled on

Town founder Mary E. (Foote) Miller and her husband, DeLafayette "Lafe" Miller, in 1863. *Lafayette Public Library*.

a homestead near Haystack Mountain north of Boulder. George and Sarah returned to Iowa in 1861 or 1862 to gather their belongings. In May 1862, they set out once more for Colorado Territory with a herd of fifty dairy cows.

Hot on the heels of the Churches, newlyweds Lafe and Mary Elizabeth (Foote) Miller, who had met each other because they were rural neighbors in Independence, set out via wagon train from their Iowa home in 1863 in search of opportunity in the same region the Churches had explored.

Journeying into new frontiers came naturally for Lafe, whose father, John, helped found Toulon, Illinois, in the early 1840s. Ancestors of Lafe's mother, also Mary, were missionaries in South Africa.

Both the Millers and the Churches made an impact from the get-go: the Churches, for their stagecoach swing station on Ben Holladay's Overland Stage Line, now the burgeoning Church Ranch commercial area off U.S. Highway 36; the Millers, for their early foray into operating a saloon, the Rock Creek Tavern, about two miles south of the current Lafayette and five miles north of Church's stop, for their impact on early politics and commerce in Boulder and for Mary's founding of the saloon-free community of Lafayette in 1888.

THE GENERIC NAMES *FAYETTE* and *Lafayette* are derived from a Revolutionary War general whose full name was Marie Joseph Paul Yves Roch Gilbert du Motier, the Marquis de la Fayette (Lafayette). General Lafayette, an ardent supporter of emancipation, was a French aristocrat who helped George Washington defeat the British. Lafayette commanded Continental army troops at the 1871 Battle of Yorktown.

Cities and counties in the United States named after the Marquis de Lafayette include Fayette County, Indiana; Fayette County, Pennsylvania; Fayetteville, North Carolina; Lafayette, California; Lafayette, Louisiana; Lafayette, Indiana; and Lafayette, Arkansas. Interestingly, the state of Colorado was nearly named "Lafayette" when it was declared a territory in 1861.

DELAFAYETTE MILLER WAS BORN to Dr. John and Mary "Charlotte" (Able) Miller in 1840 inside a cabin built about 1835 on a tree-covered Illinois hilltop known as "Miller's Point." A few months later, on July 28, 1841, John Miller conveyed fifty acres of his farm to found the town of Toulon (pronounced "too-lahn"), the county seat of Stark County. A street in that town bears his name. In 1853, John Miller was elected justice of the peace for Toulon and served for several years as a judge in Stark County courts.

Toulon is located in north-central Illinois. Five miles to the east of Toulon is the town of La Fayette, Illinois, founded in 1836 as "Lafayette." At some point in the town's history, the name was split into its current two-word form (*La* and *Fayette*). There's no historical record of La Fayette, Illinois, being named for Marquis de Lafayette, but the correlation is fairly strong.

In late 1853, John Miller relocated his family to Independence, Buchanan County, Iowa. Lafayette Miller was a rural neighbor of Mary Foote, and the two attended the same Congregational church. Lafayette and Mary married in 1862 and ventured to Colorado in 1863.

Lafayette Miller was active in early Boulder, Colorado politics. He lost the 1878 mayoral election by four votes and was elected town trustee a month later. Lafayette and his brother-in-law James B. Foote (Mary Miller's brother) owned butcher shops in Erie and Boulder and a liquor distributorship in Boulder. Lafayette died in 1878 in Boulder at age thirty-eight. The cause of death was described in his obituary as "derangement of the liver," likely the result of overconsumption of alcohol.

1

A PEOPLES ERASED

The promise of wealth that stirred the frenzy of the late-1850s Colorado gold rush helped set the stage for our region's unimaginable prosperity. But it came at a cost.

As she was approaching her one hundredth birthday in 1946, Boulder County pioneer Eliza Buford Rothrock retold her husband, John's, first encounter with Chief Left Hand, also known as Chief Niwot, the leader of a band of Southern Arapaho that frequented Boulder Valley.

John Rothrock was a member of Captain Thomas A. Aikins's party of thirty-two gold seekers who had embarked in a wagon train from Omaha and Nebraska City with a destination of Cherry Creek. The train followed the south fork of the Platte River, but Aikins's group veered west at the St. Vrain River to seek fortune on their own in the foothills north of Denver City.

John Rothrock said that the group, considered the Boulder Valley's first White campers, had arrived on the "17th day of October in 1858 at a place called 'Red Rocks' on Boulder Creek," an area now known as Settler's Park at the mouth of Boulder Canyon. The following week, they began felling trees and building log cabins.

Left Hand, who had learned English in his youth from trappers and mountain men who crisscrossed the Front Range, greeted the prospectors but strongly objected to the settlers building cabins on the Arapaho bands'

Arapaho camp near Cheyenne, Wyoming, circa 1870, by William S. Soule. *National Anthropological Archives, Smithsonian Institution, 01156800.*

traditional winter refuge. Aikins maintained that the gold seekers would only be wintering in Boulder Canyon, not settling permanently. According to John Rothrock, the Aikins party "gave him gifts and fed him some good meals and told him he was our great advisor, our big chief, too. So Left Hand said we would be brothers and we could stay."

Though not their ancestral home, the Arapahos' territory was shared with Cheyenne and Sioux and included about eighty thousand square miles from the Arkansas River in today's southern Colorado north to North Platte River in Wyoming. Combined, the Arapaho and Cheyenne included about five thousand men, women and children. To the west and southwest of their territory were the Utes, and to the northeast were the Pawnees, both longtime enemies of the Arapaho and Cheyenne. Wanting to avoid conflict, Left Hand let the Red Rocks prospectors go about their business.

Bear Head, another Southern Arapaho, did not agree with Left Hand and wanted the prospectors gone. A few days later, Bear Head dreamed that a great flood had washed the Indians away but the White man's cabin remained. Bear Head took this as a sign that the Great Spirit did not want the White man disturbed, and he allowed the prospectors to build. With this, Aikins assured Chief Left Hand that the group would camp for the winter then move on.

By December 1859, only thirteen of the original thirty-two gold seekers remained; the other nineteen had returned East. In January 1859, several men from the Aikins party discovered gold twelve miles up Boulder Canyon. By February 1859, Aikins had reneged on his promise to Left Hand and organized and platted the Boulder City Town Company. Later that year, John Rothrock surveyed the public square and platted the first one hundred lots along Pearl Street.

In February 1859, Left Hand's band of Arapaho moved from Boulder City north to St. Vrain Canyon.

Aikins, going back on his word in 1859, epitomizes the mistreatment that the Arapaho and Cheyenne would endure for decades to come.

John Rothrock homesteaded land in 1860 along Boulder Creek where U.S. Highway 287 crosses and became a successful businessman in Longmont. Eliza Buford Rothrock's father operated the stage stop at the Boulder Creek crossing in the late 1860s. The Rothrocks' next-door neighbor, pioneer Anthony Arnett, brought the first one hundred heifers to Boulder Valley in 1870, donated land for the University of Colorado in 1872 and went on to guide the development of Boulder in its formative years.

Left Hand was killed on November 29, 1864, at the Sand Creek massacre in eastern Colorado. His body was never found, but a firsthand account of the battle by Colorado Cavalry volunteer Morse H. Coffin indicates that Left Hand sustained a severe leg injury and was carried from the battlefield. There are no known photos of Left Hand.

One of the most patient and optimistic people to ever inhabit the Boulder Valley, Left Hand held an unswerving belief that everything would work out for the best. He believed that fighting the White man with weapons would only bring greater numbers of White soldiers with technologically superior weapons. He believed that his people could adapt to the onslaught of settlers, who were wiping out the buffalo herds the Arapaho lived off, by returning the tribe to their agrarian roots. In the years that followed his first encounter with the Boulder City settlers, Left Hand simply wanted a place for his tribe to call its own, and he wanted, above all, for the White men he trusted to keep their promises.

THE STEADY ADVANCEMENT OF the White man into Indian Territory in 1860 and 1861 caused the Plains Indians to form an alliance. Sioux, Apache, Kiowa, Arapaho, Comanche and Cheyenne banded together to close down migrant traffic on the Oregon Trail. In 1862, the Overland Mail and Express Company abandoned its segment that ran from North Platte to Sweetwater via Fort Laramie and rerouted stagecoaches south from Fort Kearney in Nebraska along the South Platte River to roughly where today's Greeley is located. In 1864, stagecoaches were rerouted even farther south and through Denver, then north along the Cherokee Trail (and through what is now Lafayette) to reconnect with the Overland Trail on the Laramie plains (near what is now Laramie, Wyoming).

After the 1864 Sand Creek massacre, Sioux, Arapaho and Cheyenne moved north of the North Platte River. Angered by the death of an estimated two hundred to three hundred persons, mostly women and children, at the hands of Colonel John M. Chivington, the tribes waged all-out war along the South Platte River and in eastern Colorado. Stage stations and ranches were pillaged and burned, migrant wagon trains were attacked and U.S. Army outposts were harassed.

THE HISTORY OF THE Arapaho and Cheyenne has been written largely through the biased and observational filter of the White man. One exception is the late-1800s narrative of the Cheyenne and Arapaho written by George Bent, the son of Colonel William Bent (who built Bent's Fort) and of Owl Woman, a Southern Cheyenne. George Bent assimilated into the Cheyenne tribe and, starting in 1863, fought as a Cheyenne warrior in an alliance of Sioux, Arapaho and Cheyenne. Bent fought alongside prominent Cheyenne warriors Roman Nose, Dull Knife and Little Wolf; Sioux warriors Red Cloud, Young Man Afraid of His Horses, Little Wound, Old Man Afraid of His Horses and Crazy Horse; and Chief Black Bear of the Arapaho. Red Cloud led his warriors in the successful 1866–68 effort to close the Bozeman Trail to commercial and migrant traffic.

The Cheyenne originated in New England and are first heard of in Minnesota about 1750. In 1790, they were living on the Missouri River, joined with the Arapaho in the Black Hills and moved southward along the eastern side of the Rockies, including Colorado's Front Range, starting in the early 1800s. The Great Sioux Nation was east of Arapaho and Cheyenne lands and ranged from the Republican River in Kansas north to Canada. Although horses were reintroduced into North America by Spanish conquistadors in the 1519 (native horse species became extinct about ten thousand years ago), the Cheyenne did not secure horses until the tribe migrated into the Black Hills, about 1790.

Cheyenne and Arapaho formally occupied the area between the North Platte River and the Arkansas River after defeating the Kiowas in the late 1830s.

The Southern Arapaho took refuge each winter in this place we now call the Front Range. The tribe depended on and followed the migrating buffalo herds—estimated at more than twenty million head—in Nebraska and northern Kansas, then retreated south to low-lying valleys during the winter to escape the brutal northeast winter winds that swept the treeless plains. Boulder Valley, St. Vrain Valley and the South Platte River along what is now Denver were favored areas for the Southern Arapaho, places where the small tribe could hunker down and survive on stores of buffalo killed during the previous summer and fall.

The 1851 Fort Laramie Treaty set aside all land between the North Platte River and the Arkansas River, including the Front Range of what would become Colorado, under ownership of the Arapaho and Cheyenne. In 1855, the Kansas territorial legislature ignored the Fort Laramie Treaty and designated the area around Denver City, named after then–territory governor of Kansas, James W. Denver, as Arapahoe County.

Then the flood of gold seekers started. An estimated 150,000 White settlers set out across the plains and through Indian territory in the summer of 1859. One-third turned back before reaching the Pikes Peak area, while the remainder arrived in Denver City, Boulder City and the mountain areas. An estimated 25,000 to 35,000 stayed in the area to become settlers. By March 1860, Denver City numbered 2,000 White settlers, with an estimated 34,000 White settlers in the gold region. Settlers outnumbered the Indians by about three to one.

The 1861 Fort Wise Treaty voided the Laramie Treaty and reduced the area set aside for the Indians to just seventy square miles on either side of the Arkansas River extending from roughly today's Pueblo east to the Kansas border. In exchange for $450,000 paid over fifteen years, the Indians would cede their Laramie Treaty lands and relocate to the slice of inhospitable land with very little game.

The U.S. government assured Left Hand and the Southern Arapaho that support would be provided to help them raise crops on the Colorado reservation. But the government payments were few and far between. Over the next three years, chiefs of the Arapaho and Cheyenne tried their best to control their disillusioned and increasingly angry warriors.

A second great wave of migration occurred in 1863–64 along the South Platte River route as a large number of men headed west out of fear of being drafted and forced into the army. The Civil War also meant that the U.S. government had almost no troops for the Plains, and thus no mechanism to enforce any treaty.

By 1864, an anxious John Evans, territorial governor of Colorado, had convinced the War Department that an Indian uprising was eminent.

On June 11, 1864, the Nathan W. Hungate family was killed by Indians on their farm twenty-five miles east of Denver. In August 1864, Evans issued a proclamation advising citizens to "hunt down the Indians and to kill every hostile one they might meet."

On August 21, 1864, permission was given to Evans to raise and arm the volunteer Third Regiment, Colorado Cavalry, led by Colonel John M. Chivington, a former Methodist preacher who had no formal military training. Captain David Nichols, a former Boulder County sheriff, signed up one hundred Boulder volunteers, including prominent Boulder pioneers Granville Berkley and James Arbuthnot and Longmont pioneer William Dickens. Recruitment posters promised volunteers "all the horses and plunder taken from the Indians." Volunteers for the poorly equipped Third utilized their own weapons, but some were issued horses and ammunition. By early September, they were fully organized and ready for action.

In late September, Major Edward W. Wynkoop, a U.S. officer, gathered Cheyenne and Arapaho chiefs Black Kettle, Bull Bear, White Antelope, Neva, Bosse, Heap of Buffalo and Na-ta-nee and brought them to Denver's Camp Weld to meet with Evans. Holding a false belief that troops would not attack, the chiefs returned to the eastern Colorado plains.

On November 29, 1864, Colonel Chivington, commanding about seven hundred volunteers that included the First and Third Regiments, Colorado Cavalry, surprised an encampment of Cheyenne and Arapaho on Sand Creek. The Indians had surrendered most of their weapons days before at nearby Fort Lyon and believed they were under protection of the United States flag. In a daylong battle, Chivington's troops killed women, children and elderly men and scalped or mutilated numerous bodies in the Indian camp. Cheyenne warrior George Bent survived the massacre with a bullet wound to the hip.

After the volunteers were received as heroes in Denver, the horrific details of their actions at Sand Creek led to a congressional investigation and repudiation of the act.

Group portrait of the Camp Weld Council, Denver, Colorado, shows White and Native American (Arapaho and Cheyenne) men. *Left to right, kneeling*: Major Edward Wynkoop and Captain Silas S. Soule; *seated*: White Antelope, Bull Bear, Black Kettle, Neva and Na-ta-nee; *standing*: unidentified, Dexter Colley, John Smith, Heap of Buffalo, Bosse, Amos Steck and unidentified. *Denver Public Library, Western History Collection, X-32079.*

Repercussions included Governor Evans being stripped of his federal appointment as territorial governor. Chivington left the military in February 1865 to avoid prosecution. After brief stints in Nebraska and Ohio, Chivington returned to Denver in 1882, serving as a city sanitary inspector and undersheriff. He later was elected coroner for Denver and was once accused of taking money from pockets of the dead. He died in 1894 and is buried in Fairmount Cemetery in Denver.

IF HISTORY REMEMBERS LEFT Hand as the most trusting chief, then Chief Colorow of the Southern Utes is certainly the most traveled.

Confined to mostly South Park and southeast Colorado because of conflicts with the Arapaho, the void left by the exit of the Arapaho circa 1865 meant that Colorow and the Utes could venture far and wide—so much so that there are tales of encounters with Colorow from the Front Range west to Utah, south into New Mexico and north into Wyoming.

Colorow, Ute chief, by
William Henry Jackson.
*Denver Public Library, Western
History Collection, Z-166.*

The chief and his band of Southern Utes are known to have regularly visited Mary Miller at the Rock Creek House/Miller Tavern south of today's Lafayette, asking for biscuits and flour. Since flour was at a premium, the settlers could usually offer only cornmeal.

Mary Miller's grandson Ralph Clinton Miller Sr. (1898–1982) said in 1971 that Native Americans visited area settlers and "would do nothing but take it [corn meal] and dump it on the ground. They 'no want.' They wanted white flour."

The Waneka stage stop on Coal Creek, two miles north of the Millers' tavern, was also a favored resting spot for bands of Native Americans, including a recorded visit by a band of 1,700 Utes in 1871. Charles "Chuck" Waneka, a descendant of pioneer settler Adolf Waneka (1826–1896), had in his collection an 1865 U.S. Cavalry sword left hanging in the trees adjacent to the stop by a visiting group of Native Americans.

RALPH CLINTON MILLER SR. said that when early settlers in the area "got an Indian scare they would pick up and go to [Fort Lyon at] Sand Creek. They'd go down there, stay two or three days, and then they'd come home."

A necessity of the frontier was that the head of the household was sometimes away for weeks at a time—either mining in the foothills or helping distant neighbors cut hay—and had to leave the family behind to tend to things and, if needed, make their own way to safety.

A 1907 *Lafayette Leader* story about Mary Miller reported that "she made the 'run' from Burlington [Longmont] to Valmont with a six-month-old babe in her arms. At Valmont was located a settlers' fort, whither she went for assistance to resist an Indian attack." This would have been in 1863 and 1864, when the Millers homesteaded east of Longmont.

As late as 1868, settlers around Lafayette had contact with Indian war parties. Eliza Buford Rothrock, who homesteaded along Boulder Creek near today's U.S. Highway 287, recalled that "in 1868, the second year of our marriage, John [her husband] went to work for the Wells, Fargo & Company carrying freight between Denver and Cheyenne. One evening when I was driving the cow in to milk I saw a bunch of Indians coming toward the cabin. I hurried to the cabin and then the Indians surrounded it, demanding food. They were decorated in war paint and were a wild looking lot! I fed them all I could find in the way of cold biscuit and meat and then they left. But a few days later they came back from their Indian battle with human scalps tied about their waists and hanging from the manes of the ponies. Some of them were still dripping blood on the horses' shoulders. That's almost more than I could stand!"

2

CULTIVATING THE
WIDE-OPEN SPACES

The area's first settlers established the agricultural economy of Boulder County. The vocation is much less visible today.

THE FIRST RECORDED EVIDENCE of migrant settlers near Lafayette or Louisville was made by General Land Office surveyor Hiram Witter, who wrote in his September 1864 survey notebook that between Sections 16 and 17 of Township 1 South, Range 69 West, there was a "fence that comes E, a Log House with chimney on the section line, Coal Creek course N 60° E, and another fence, course N 45° E."

It's likely that the log cabin that Witter described was Adolf Waneka's. Witter was charged with staking section corners used for the General Land Office's public land sales, which Waneka later utilized to claim the land he'd homesteaded. The log fence in Sections 16 and 17 shows on Witter's 1864 General Land Office subdivision survey map. Other than wagon roads (trails), the fence is the only man-made object drawn on the map.

IN 1861, COAL CREEK Valley settler Henry Adolf Waneka (also spelled Waenchi, Waeneke and Waeneche) was busy building a fence. Among the first White settlers to arrive in what would become today's south Louisville (about where the modern railroad tracks cross Coal Creek off Ninety-Fifth Street), Waneka staked his land claim and commenced felling

William Barrowman, seated on a horse-drawn reaper, and sons harvesting wheat in a field near Lafayette, about 1905. The Barrowmans owned several tracts of land along East Baseline Road and South Boulder Road. *Lafayette Miners Museum.*

cottonwood trees cut from the edges of Coal Creek. He assembled a log cabin—complete with a dirt roof, clapboard door and elaborate stone fireplace—on the south bank of the creek, then fashioned an oblong half-mile-diameter stacked log fence enclosure. His fence, used to hold dairy cattle, was large enough to encompass parts of what would later become Sections 8, 9, 16 and 17 in Township 1 South. The fence, most likely made of trees stacked horizontally in a "Z" pattern, ran parallel to Coal Creek and encircled the cabin he built for he and his wife, Anna, and their three children, Anna, Henry and William.

Part of the wave of prospectors that poured into then–Kansas Territory starting in 1859, gold seeker Adolf Waneka and his family arrived together via a mule train in 1861.

Charles C. "Clancy" Waneka (1911–2005), great-grandson of Adolf Waneka, wrote in the 1990 book *Lafayette, Colorado History: Treeless Plain to Thriving City* that Adolf arrived from Connecticut in 1860 (and lived in a cave along Coal Creek), then Anna came separately with children in 1861. Clancy's cousin Charles "Chuck" Waneka (1921–2018) doubted that the family traveled separately, because in the 1860s, it was uncommon for a woman and her young children to travel on a wagon train by themselves. Researcher Jennie E. Stewart wrote in 1946 that "Adolph and Anna

Left: Adolf Waneka. *Right*: Anna Waneka. *Waneka family collection.*

Waneka…in 1861 arrived in Boulder County, taking up land near the present site of Lafayette."

In 1932, the Boulder Fourth of July Committee asked Henry "Boye" Waneka and Anna Waneka Thomas, two of Adolf's three children, about the family's pioneer history. Both said that the family came as one unit to Colorado Territory in 1861 "over the Plains with mule teams." Anna Thomas spelled her father's name "Adolph" on the 1932 questionnaire, while Boye spelled it "Adolf."

Clancy Waneka, who spelled Adolf's name with an "f," also wrote in 1990 that his great-grandfather built a cabin "east of a cave along the south bank of what is now Coal Creek southwest of Lafayette."

Adolf's land south of Louisville, which was purchased via private sale and patented at the General Land Office in Denver City in 1866, is described as "the East Half of the North East quarter of section Seventeen, and the South East quarter of the South East quarter of section Eight…containing 120 acres." In modern terms, this would be a half-mile swath of land in Louisville along the west side of Ninety-Fifth Street (Highway 42) from Dillon Road to just north of Pine Street.

With the exception of a log cabin and irrigation ditch built by a settler—possibly Langford R. Wilson, who came to Colorado in 1859—in the south portion of the adjacent Section 18, near today's Coal Creek Golf Course, there were no signs of settlers within about a five-mile radius of Wanekas. To the southeast of Wanekas on the banks of Rock Creek was the Dow Road House, which offered meals to settlers, prospectors, teamsters driving freight wagons and regional stagecoaches running north–south along the Front Range. To the north, along Boulder Creek, were the feisty Great Western Land Claim Association settlers.

Adolf's extensive stacked log fence served two purposes. It kept his herd of dairy cattle from straying, so that they could be easily rounded up and milked for butter and cheese. It also kept cattle rustlers from easily running off with a stray. Trying to steal cattle late at night would have meant disassembling the heavy log fence—not a good work-versus-reward ratio. Plains Indians, especially the Pawnee, often built corrals from logs stacked horizontally so that rival tribes would have difficulty stealing a warrior's best horses.

Waneka family records indicate that Adolf and Anna established their permanent homestead and stagecoach stop south of Lafayette as early as 1862 on Section 10, where Coal Creek bisects today's U.S. Highway 287 in Lafayette. This was about one mile east of Sections 16 and 17 in south Louisville. In 1872, Adolf Waneka was awarded a homestead patent for his Lafayette land under the terms of the 1862 Homestead Act.

On a late summer morning in September 1864, the crew of five General Land Office surveyors led by Hiram Witter spent several hours on the north bank of Coal Creek scampering back and forth across Adolf Waneka's log fence—up one side, then down the other. The surveying crew would have been visible to Adolf and Anna few days earlier as they measured the higher ridges above the south bank of Coal Creek.

The government survey party's job in 1864 was to establish and then map the subdivision lines that defined the thirty-six sections in the thirty-six-square-mile Township 1 South. The township corners for most of the Front Range had been staked the previous summer by government surveyor George E. Pierce. Witter, a deputy surveyor for the U.S. Surveyor General's Office in Denver, was the compass man, also known as a transitman or "chief of party." He had four helpers: Frederick Barnard and Samuel Montgomery, who were the chainmen (the men who stretched out the sixty-six-foot measuring tape, the length being two chains); William Sallyards, who was the mound builder (the man who built or buried the survey monument after the chainman had staked it out); and James Johnston, the flagman (the man who held the level rod so that the compass man could keep the chainmen going in a straight line).

Surveying is a process of establishing reference points or boundaries on a piece of land. In their 1864 survey records for Township 1 South, which is where most of today's Lafayette and Louisville sits, surveyors described references points, called monuments, that they placed on the ground. Corners where sections intersected were often marked with a charred tree branch, a rectangular piece of sandstone or a stack of rocks. The surveyors were instructed to make notations about natural and man-made features along the survey line (streams or rivers, vegetation) and general land features (flat plains, rolling hills, steep bluffs). They also described the quality of the soil and its suitability for farming, ranking it from first class to third class. Most of the southwest corner of Township 1 South, the area around U.S. 36 and McCaslin Boulevard in Superior, was described as second- and third-class soil, unbroken and hard with lots of rocks.

When the surveyor encountered or observed man-made features such as trails, fences, irrigation ditches and structures, he made note of it. The Coal Creek Valley surveyors were so impressed with Adolf Waneka's fence on Sections 8, 9, 16 and 17 that it's mentioned several times in their notes and is shown on 1864 government maps. It was almost compulsory that surveyors show Adolf's fence on the map—they'd spent too much time climbing up and over the hefty obstruction trying to get their section lines established.

THE ACME HAY RICKER AND LOADER.

The Acme Ricker, a spring-loaded device that stacked hay that was powered by horses. Pacific Rural Press, *February 16, 1884.*

Remains of a ricker abandoned in a field off Aspen Ridge Drive in Lafayette, 2020. *Photo by the author.*

The 1864 government surveyors noted the north–south Cherokee Trail stage road running through Section 10 and labeled it "Laramie Road." The Section 10 survey notes and maps didn't indicate the presence of improvements such as ditches, fences or structures, but survey notes did state: "In the Valley of Coal Creek, there is good farming land with small growth of cottonwood and willow."

The Township 1 South surveyors describe the area farther south of Section 10, around today's Rock Creek Farm (formerly Stearns Dairy), as land "claimed by actual settlers." This was most likely a reference to Thomas J. Lindsey, who was running the Rock Creek House tavern.

Immigration reached its peak in 1907, when 1,285,000 immigrant entries were recorded. By 1910, 13,345,000 foreign-born persons were living in the United States.

3

A TOWN TAKES SHAPE

The influx of White settlers turned the treeless prairie into platted towns with streets, houses and thriving centers of commerce.

TWENTY THREE-YEAR-OLD DELAFAYETTE "LAFE" Miller and nineteen-year-old Mary E. (Foote) Miller arrived in Colorado Territory in late August 1863, settling on land the two had purchased on the banks of the St. Vrain River east of Burlington, now Longmont. From Independence, Iowa, Lafe and Mary set out south in late May 1863 with three wagons pulled by twelve (or more) oxen en route to Joplin, Missouri. They then headed west to Denver City along the Smoky Hill Trail, considered "the central route" and most difficult of the migrant trails into Colorado. The "easier" routes, the northern and southern routes, followed the South Platte River and Arkansas River, respectively.

Two of the three fifty-square-foot wagons the Millers piloted contained a multipiece thresher, the first thresher brought to Boulder County. The Millers also brought wheat seeds with them, but the two arrived in Colorado Territory late in the growing season, which meant they couldn't plant—and had nothing to harvest.

Frank Miller (1893–1973), Lafayette and Mary Miller's grandson, said in 1968 that the thresher—powered by two horses and used to separate the wheat grain from the chaff—was freighted out of Missouri on wagons, in pieces. One piece would have been the horse tread, a device that allowed

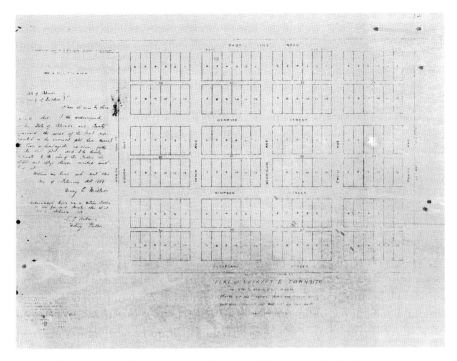

Mary Miller's plat of Lafayette townsite, February 1888. *Lafayette Public Library.*

two horses to walk in place to power the thresher. The second piece would have been the grain separator, connected by a continuous belt to the horse treadmill. The thresher operated on the ground, but for transport both pieces were sized to fit in a wagon box and would have been slid onto the wagon using wood timbers.

In early September 1863, after the wheat in fields near St. Vrain Canyon had been cut by a horse-drawn reaper and bundled into shocks—so that the bundles could be carried to the thresher—Lafe and his brother-in-law George Henry Church (1830–1918) climbed onto the wagons hauling the newly arrived threshing machine and set out westward from Burlington for the mouth of St. Vrain Canyon.

Boulder County pioneer Morse H. Coffin (1836–1913), who homesteaded near what would become Lyons, said in his 1911 memoir that he hired out the Millers' thresher for harvest. "Our first grain, wheat and oats, was raised in 1863, and this crop was threshed by Lafe Miller and Henry Church, for which we paid them 25 cents per bushel," said Coffin. "We sold some of these oats at home for 15 cents per pound."

Like Coffin, George Henry Church came to Colorado Territory several years before the Millers and had located near Mount Vernon Canyon, where he and his wife, Sarah (Miller) Church, had attempted to run a dairy. But the milk cows didn't fare well, so in early 1863, the couple moved to Haystack Mountain, on land north of what is now Boulder. Church was one of the first Colorado settlers to use dryland wheat-farming techniques and would have easily sold Lafe Miller on the idea of "farming out" his threshing machine to area wheat growers.

As explained in earlier chapters of this book, the Churches probably convinced the Millers to venture west. Sarah Church was Lafe's sister, and George had worked for Lafe and Sarah's father, John, back in Iowa. In 1864, George Henry Church bought the Millers' acreage near Burlington, and the Millers moved south ten miles to operate a saloon, tavern and stage stop, built by Dr. James E. Dow and owned by Thomas J. Lindsey, on land along Rock Creek patented by Mary's brother James B. Foote. The Churches probably influenced this move as well, since they also acquired and operated the former Child's stage stop near what is now Church Ranch on U.S. Highway 36, about five miles south of Dow's roadhouse.

Lafe's sister Sarah Church described in the family history piece "History of the Church Ranch and Church Family" the countryside in the years before the Millers arrived. Sarah wrote in her diary that the Church Ranch stage stop was "Five miles from any other house…not one till you reached Rock Creek where Dr. Daw [Dow] was entertaining the travelers, [then] open country to the Platte River."

FRANK MILLER COMMENTED IN 1968 that Lafe and Mary Miller and her brother James B. Foote and his wife, Harriet, shared a home straddling the center section line of Section 2 on the south side of Baseline Road in what is now Lafayette. This was the early 1870s Foote-Miller Farm, later known as the Miller Farm and the Willow Glenn Farm. Most of the Footes lived on the east side of the house, and the Millers, along with Mary's dad, John B. Foote, lived on the west side. James B. Foote had applied for a homestead patent for his land, so the Footes were required to live on their homestead land for five years in order to receive the government-issued patent. Because Lafayette and Mary Miller purchased the adjacent (northwest) acreage from Francis P. Heatley and Edward Chase, the Millers owned their land outright and weren't required to "homestead." So, the split Foote-Miller "condo" that straddled the one-fourth sections

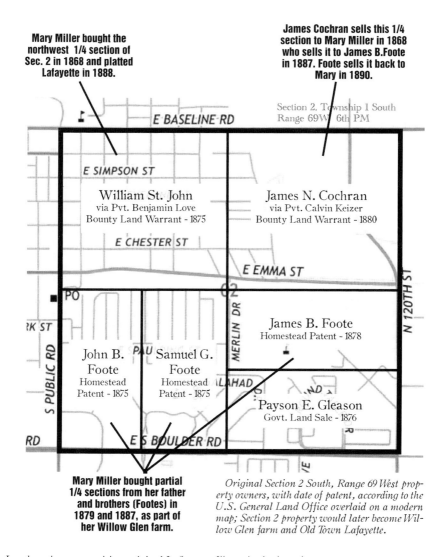

Mary Miller bought the northwest 1/4 section of Sec. 2 in 1868 and platted Lafayette in 1888.

James Cochran sells this 1/4 section to Mary Miller in 1868 who sells it to James B.Foote in 1887. Foote sells it back to Mary in 1890.

Section 2, Township 1 South Range 69W 6th PM

E BASELINE RD

E SIMPSON ST

William St. John
via Pvt. Benjamin Love
Bounty Land Warrant - 1875

James N. Cochran
via Pvt. Calvin Keizer
Bounty Land Warrant - 1880

E CHESTER ST

E EMMA ST

PO

John B. Foote
Homestead Patent - 1875

Samuel G. Foote
Homestead Patent - 1875

James B. Foote
Homestead Patent - 1878

Payson E. Gleason
Govt. Land Sale - 1876

E S BOULDER RD

Mary Miller bought partial 1/4 sections from her father and brothers (Footes) in 1879 and 1887, as part of her Willow Glen farm.

Original Section 2 South, Range 69 West property owners, with date of patent, according to the U.S. General Land Office overlaid on a modern map; Section 2 property would later become Willow Glen farm and Old Town Lafayette.

Land sections comprising original Lafayette. *Illustration by the author.*

was probably an economic consideration for the Millers rather than a requirement prescribed by the Homestead Act.

The prospect of striking it rich with a gold-mining claim brought tens of thousands of settlers to Colorado Territory in the 1860s. Lafe and Mary Miller had gold fever, too.

Starting in 1867, Lafe Miller and brother-in-law and business partner James B. Foote had interests in several mining claims in Gold Hill, including the Nip & Tuck Lode, Monumental City Lode, National Debt Lode, Silver Bell Lode, Melbourne Lode, Little Minnie Lode and Truthful William Lode. During the 1860s and 1870s, it was not unusual for settlers to farm in the summer months and then spend the rest of the year working the silver or gold claims in the foothills above Boulder City.

Although there's no evidence that Lafe Miller mined gold, we do know that the Millers made a good living by providing food and supplies for gold seekers. Lafe Miller and James B. Foote raised their own cattle at the Rock Creek House/Miller Tavern Ranch starting in 1866. Miller and Foote registered the "RC" brand with the Boulder County Clerk and Recorder in 1869. The two also ran two meat shops, one in Boulder, known as Miller & Company, and one in Erie that was built in 1871. James B. Foote operated the markets until 1883. The Millers also grew and cut hay at Rock Creek, then hauled it about forty miles to Black Hawk, where it was sold to miners. Hay delivered to the mountains could fetch from $300 to $500 a ton. The Millers also sold butter and eggs in Black Hawk and Central City.

ONE OF TOWN FOUNDER Mary Miller's most important and unsung accomplishments was helping women achieve financial independence. During her stints as real estate agent and part owner of both the Farmers' & Miners' State Bank, which failed in 1898, and the Lafayette Bank, which she formed in 1900, she often lent money and signed the property deed over to the female of the household rather than the male. This was not a common occurrence in the era of American Victorianism, when women had limited legal rights and didn't have the right to vote in Colorado until 1893. Boys went to school and girls stayed home to learn domestic skills. The man of the house earned the wages and engaged in politics. The woman stayed home, kept house and raised the children.

In 1888 and 1889, Mary Miller platted eighty-nine acres of her farm into 353 Old Town lots and recognized an opportunity to empower her fellow sistren. From 1888 to 1904, 50 of the 190 purchased lots were sold to women, some for as little as one dollar. Boulder County property records show Old Town lots, 50 feet by 140 feet, sold to men at an average price of about ninety dollars. The purchase price for lots sold to women averaged about forty-eight dollars.

Many of the women who received the lots—for as little as $1 to $5—were Mary's friends who attended the Congregational church. Hattie Simpson,

John H. Simpson's wife, bought two lots for $1 each. Hannah Stobs and Louise McClane each received a lot for $1. Martha Fishback paid $5. Caroline Moon and Sarah Van Etten bought lots for $50 each, while Jennie Harrison was charged $25. Mary's best friend, Grace Cannon, bought several lots for $75 each.

Clarissa Jane (Ewing) Hobart, Hannah Briggs, Mary (Simpson) Scott, Margaret Simpson, Joanna Metcalf, Dell May Cannon, Annie Carr, Selma Lowman, Isabelle Bell, Sarah Blackwill, Ella Wylam, Matilda Noble, Margaret Abernethy and Ruth Hopkins were charged from $75 to $100 per lot.

In nearby Louisville, where Louis Nawatny platted the town in 1878, the original town lots had sold out by 1891. Nawatny platted sixty-six lots along Front Street and Second Street (now Main Street). By 1891, all sixty-six lots were sold, forty-seven to men and nineteen to women. Future Lafayette residents Walter W. Moon and John H. Simpson both purchased Louisville lots from Nawatny. Most of his lots sold for around $100, and women didn't receive a discount.

What follows are the street names for Mary Miller's 1888 plat (thirty-seven acres with 144 lots):

> **Gough Avenue** (a person) named for national temperance leader John B. Gough.
> **Finch Avenue** (a person) named for Prohibition National Committee chairman and Good Templar organizer John B. Finch (1852–1887).
> **Foote Avenue** (family relation) named after Mary Miller's father, John B. Foote.
> **Simpson Street** (family relation) named for John H. Simpson, a temperance ally of Mary Miller's who sank the Spencer-Simpson Mine (1887–89).
> **Iowa Avenue** (the state) where Lafayette and Mary Miller were married.
> **Michigan Avenue** (the state) where Mary Miller spent part of her childhood.
> **Geneseo Street** (city) where Mary Miller was born, Geneseo, New York.
> **Cleveland Street** (city) named for Cleveland, Ohio, but possibly for Democratic president Grover Cleveland.

The street names added by Mary Miller in the 1889 Town of Lafayette replat (eighty-nine acres with 353 lots) are as follows:

> **Harrison Avenue** *(a person) named after Republican president Benjamin Harrison, a supporter of the temperance movement.*
> **Chester Street** *(a person) named after Republican president Chester A. Arthur.*
> **Cannon Street** *(family relation) named for George B. Cannon (and possibly Grace Cannon), a temperance ally of Mary Miller.*
> **Emma Street** *(family relation) Mary Miller's favorite niece, Emma (McClane) Rabb.*

Mary Miller was austere, fastidious, benevolent, principled and, above all, tough. A modest woman, she shied from the spotlight. There's only one known newspaper interview in which she is quoted, one authored in 1912 by *Boulder County Miner* reporter Stuart Elizabeth Loyd.

Her love for her husband, Lafe, is evident in her committing part of her farmland to the town, platting it with Boulder County and then naming it "Lafayette." After Lafe Miller's death in 1878, Mary raised her six children by herself and later moved from Willow Glenn Farm to a modest, one-story home she built at East Cleveland and Michigan Streets.

Always willing to help the downtrodden, Mary noted that, starting in 1910, the large coal camps forced employees into on-site rental housing that sucked the life out of the laborers. Henceforth, if a local coal miner and his family wanted a home to call their own, she lent the money and accommodated months-late mortgage payments when hard times set in during the frequent strikes.

Like other area pioneers—Harmons, Wanekas, Willises, Schofields—Mary Miller hired a schoolmaster and made room in her farmhouse parlor so that her and her neighbors' kids could get an education. After platting and incorporating the town, Mary helped procure Lafayette's first public school (for its twenty-four students), located in a house on East Cleveland Street. Then she hired and paid the salary of the first teacher, Mrs. Scott. When the high school sports teams needed practice fields, she built them on the family farm. When the new school district needed a school board president, she gladly stepped into the role. When the fledgling coal mines needed new rights-of-way for railroad spurs, she saw to it that the railroad companies got the land.

When the town needed a bank, she started one. When that one failed, she started another one. When the town needed a general store, she helped start one and often gave away food from its inventory to families in need. She was one of the first in town to install a newfangled invention called the telephone.

When the town needed its first church, she donated the land, funded the $3,000 cost of construction for the Congregational church and paid the preacher's salary. When Methodist parishioners needed land to build a new church, she made sure they got it. When the town needed a new flour mill, she loaned the money to build it, then helped manage it. When the town needed an electric generation plant on the east side of town, she leased the land and loaned the money for the equipment. When that power plant became outdated, she saw to it that a new state-of-the art power plant was built by East Coast investors on land she owned at Waneka Lake. When a severe cold-weather snap hit the Eastern Plains of Colorado, she secured and shipped 175 railroad cars filled with donated coal.

Mary Miller's benevolence is tempered by her exclusion from the town of persons of color, a racial bias publicly displayed by early town residents, coal miners, union organizations and the coal mine operators. Of the over four hundred town lots that Miller owned, Boulder County Clerk and Recorder records show that none were sold to anyone other than Whites.

Mary Miller died in 1921, and the Miller family lost the Willow Glenn Farm at the start of the Great Depression in 1929. Nothing remains of the farm, but her modest home at 409 East Cleveland still stands. One of the handful of times she was mentioned in the local newspaper was a December 1914 *Lafayette Leader* item that summarized in a few words her astonishingly benevolent nature: "If the party that took the gate from Mrs. Mary E. Miller's fence on Halloween will bring it back, she will give a reward and ask no questions."

4

A TOWN BUILT ON COAL MINING

From 1888 until 1956, the coal mining industry sustained Lafayette. But the dangerous work conditions in the fourteen coal mines that once dotted the countryside in and near Lafayette took a toll.

On a hot summer day in July 1881, lawyer and coal speculator Walter H. Underwood rode up on his buggy and knocked on the door of the modest farmhouse owned by Mary Miller and her brother and sister-in-law, James B. and Harriet Foote. Underwood, who'd traveled from Gunnison County with a proposal of riches, probably read about coal discoveries north of Denver in the *Rocky Mountain News* and was anxious to prospect on what Mary Miller described as the Foote-Miller Farm, where early settlers had gathered home heating fuel from coal outcroppings.

When Underwood greeted Mary, he would have removed his hat and asked if the man of the house was available. After all, it was uncommon at the time for women to be bothered with land matters, negotiations and other "man's work." But Mary Miller's experience in buying and selling residential and commercial lots in Boulder, where she and her late husband, Lafayette, lived during most of the 1870s, would have given her the upper hand. She was no pushover, and even if her beloved husband hadn't died three years earlier, Mary still would have taken the lead in negotiating any deals with regard to the Foote-Miller Farm.

Barbara Hutchison Larson of Lafayette stands on the back of a railroad flatcar containing mostly slack coal in Dacono, circa 1918. *Lafayette Public Library, donated by James D. Hutchison.*

A month later, on August 17, 1881, Mary Miller and Harriet Foote agreed to lease Underwood coal mining rights, the first recorded coal lease for the Lafayette area, allowing him to mine up to fifteen thousand tons of coal each year from the NW 1/4 of Section 2 in Township 1S, except the S 1/2 of the SE 1/4 section, which was owned at the time by Payson Gleason. Underwood paid Miller and Foote $1,000 (the equivalent of $25,000 in 2020 dollars) up front for the lease, and Mary and Harriet agreed to split the agreed $0.07-per-ton royalty. The lease, recorded with the Boulder County Clerk and Recorder, made it clear that Underwood would have to keep his mine buildings and mining activities "at least 50 rods [800 feet] from the dwelling house" located at the very south end of Section 2 and that the gently rolling hills above the mine be "preserved for agricultural and pastural purposes."

Unfortunately for Underwood, the nearest railroad ran through Louisville, three miles west of Foote-Miller Farm and also along Coal Creek one mile to the east. Without the railroad, only enough coal could be extracted to meet the demand of locals residing in the few farmhouses dotting the prairie east of Louisville. The Colorado Central Railroad line, which would later become Colorado & Southern Railroad, had been laid down in 1873, and C.C. Welch was already extracting coal on David Kerr's land west of the Foote-Miller Farm.

The Denver, Longmont & Northwestern Railroad had also laid a narrow-gauge track east of Lafayette and to the Mitchell Mine north of Lafayette in 1881 to serve the growing coal market in Denver. That track was extended to Longmont in 1882.

But there was no railroad spur connecting the Foote-Miller Farm to the main rail lines. Coal from Underwood's enterprise destined for the Denver market would have to be delivered to the nearby train by horse and wagon, about one thousand pounds at a time.

Underwood probably tried to make the numbers work, but after the lease was signed and the cash deposited, Mary Miller and Harriet Foote would never hear from Underwood again. Fortunately for Mary and Harriet, the coal speculators would come knocking again a few years later.

The coal mines east of Lafayette, such as the Baker and Standard Mines on the hill above Coal Creek, were sunk as early as 1883. Both Frank Miller in 1968 and coal miner Elmo Lewis (1905–1979) in 1976 stated that the Cannon coal mine was the first in Lafayette proper. The *Lafayette News* and *Lafayette Leader* newspapers (founded in 1898 and 1905, respectively), described the Simpson Mine as being the first, and state mining records from the "Third Biennial Report of the Inspector of Coal Mines of the State of Colorado for the Years 1887–88" point to the Simpson Mine opening and producing coal first.

John H. Simpson, his father, James Simpson Sr., and his brothers William and Joseph leased coal rights for the Simpson Mine from James B. Foote in July 1887. For unknown reasons, the Simpsons didn't sink the first of two Simpson Mine shafts on Foote's property until early 1888 and didn't produce coal until September 1888, a few months before the Cannon Mine started producing coal. One of the initial Simpson Mine shafts was located in what is now the alley in the 800 block of East Simpson in Lafayette.

Deed and encumbrance recordings at the Boulder County Clerk and Recorder show that James B. Foote, who owned most of the land east of Foote Avenue and south of Baseline Road, signed a coal lease with James Cannon Jr., a Denver coal magnate with ties to Lafayette, in February 1888. Cannon was able to sink his coal mine, located on the south side of East Emma Street where it meets today's Merlin Drive, by October 1888.

Simpson coal mine in about 1909, owned at the time by the Northern Coal and Coke Company. *From author's collection.*

Company "Type H" housing at the Simpson coal mine, 1911. *Lafayette Public Library.*

A 1913 view of the Strathmore coal mine, located south of East Emma Street along South Public Road. *Lafayette Public Library.*

County records also show that James B. Foote borrowed $6,000 in 1888 using the Cannon lease as collateral.

John H. Simpson found coal on Mary Miller's property—west of James B. Foote's property—as early as 1884, but it wasn't until March 1889 that Mary, who at the time owned most of the land south of today's Baseline Road and west of Foote Avenue, leased coal rights to the Simpsons. The Simpsons and their partner, Charles Spencer, sank the Spencer Mine shaft two hundred yards west of the 1887 Simpson Mine shaft.

The Spencer Mine started producing coal in 1890, and its shaft was located in what is now the 700 block of East Cleveland in Lafayette. Spencer and the Simpsons agreed to pay Mary Miller twelve and a half cents per ton of lump coal in royalties and agreed not to interfere with any aboveground property in Miller's newly platted town of Lafayette.

By 1890, Charles Spencer and the Simpsons had secured a three-mile Union Pacific, Denver and Gulf Railway spur going east from the main line in Louisville to serve their respective mines, which was facilitated by Mary Miller agreeing to a railroad right-of-way on the southern end of her 1889 replat of Lafayette Old Town. (This was probably the reason she refiled her thirty-seven-acre 1888 town plat with a larger, eighty-nine-acre town plat in 1889.) The railroad company allowed the Spencer

John H. Simpson. *Lafayette Public Library*.

and Simpson Mines to reimburse the railway for construction costs and right-of-way acquisition over a period of time by charging a premium for each railroad car hauled from the mine.

At the behest of future business partner James Cannon Jr., John H. Simpson commenced right-of-way negotiations in 1890 with the Chicago, Burlington & Quincy Railroad (also known as the Burlington & Missouri) to bring an additional—and competing—rail spur to the Spencer and Simpson Mines from the CB&Q rail line east of Coal Creek on the east side of Lafayette. In February 1890, Simpson agreed to pay then-Cannon Mine owner Daniel Skinner $600 for a CB&Q right-of-way across land located south of the Spencer-Simpson Mines.

The Spencer and Simpson Mines operated as separate mines until 1893, when United Coal Company, under the direction of James Cannon Jr., combined the two into a single mine with the familiar "Simpson Mine" moniker.

State coal production records show that the Baker Mine, located on Blue Ribbon Hill east of Lafayette, started producing coal in 1883, and the adjacent Standard Mine started producing coal in 1887. Although the Simpson Coal Company sank a shaft as early as 1887, the Simpson Mine did not produce coal until late 1888, about 1,100 tons.

From 1888 to 1926, the Simpson Mine produced over four million tons of coal from a fifteen-mile subterranean network of passageways under most of original Lafayette—from Bermont Street on the west to 119th Street on the east and from the Beacon Hill subdivision on the north to Emma Street on the south.

IN 1887, COLORADO COAL production totaled 1.7 million tons. By 1892, when Lafayette mines were in full production, state coal output doubled to 3.7 million tons. In 1893, Colorado railroads hauled 3.4 million tons of coal, one-third of which went to Kansas, New Mexico, Nebraska, Nevada, Texas and Utah.

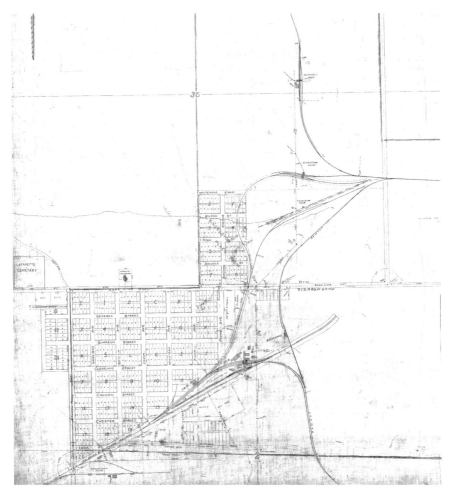

A 1909 map of Lafayette, showing the railroad spurs servicing Lafayette's many coal mines. *Lafayette Public Library*.

From 1883 to 1958, Boulder County mines produced 43,000,000 tons of coal. Peak Boulder County coal production, facilitated by twenty-five mines, occurred in 1907, when 1,399,518 tons of coal were mined. The peak number of Boulder County coal mines occurred in 1935, when twenty-seven mines were active.

LAFAYETTE HELPED MAKE DENVER what it is today. Not only did coal mined in Lafayette, Louisville, Marshall and Erie—known as the Northern Coal Field or Northern Field—heat Denver's growing number of households starting in the late 1880s, it also fueled Denver's smelters, cotton mills, breweries, paper mills, shoe factories and power plants.

In 1899, the Colorado Inspector of Coal Mines estimated that the 405-square-mile Northern Coal Field contained 2.56 billion tons of coal.

Up to the turn of the twentieth century, Denver customers consumed most of the coal mined in the area as fast it could be hauled up from the subterranean tunnels. Lafayette coal mines were wired for telephones starting in 1891, almost fifteen years before the rest of the town, because the Denver coal dealers needed a quicker way to place orders.

Archaeological evidence indicates that Hopi Indians in the Southwest used coal as early as the 1300s for making pottery and for cooking and heating. Europeans first observed coal in America in 1659, when a Jesuit missionary described the Poualak-Assiniboine tribes in today's Minnesota area burning coal for heating and cooking. In 1669, Father Hennepin, a priest traveling with French explorer Robert de La Salle, observed coal near Peoria, Illinois. Some Indians called coal "stove that will burn long forest fire," and the Sioux called coal *čhaȟlí* (pronounced "chash-uh-lee").

In 1704, Pennsylvania frontiersmen accidentally propped some black rocks next to a fire used for a cooking kettle, at which time the rocks caught fire and "burned fiercely with a bright light." The frontiersmen were scared by the fire, grabbed their kettle and fled. They agreed that the devil would show up if they stayed. The frontiersmen told their tale to Elias Blank, a Quaker who'd received land from William Penn. Blank realized the value of the black rocks, found the camp location and uncovered an extensive streamside coal seam in an area that would become an anchor for the nation's infant coal industry. After Pittsburgh was laid out, Penn was granted a charter in 1786 to mine coal in the hills surrounding the city.

During their explorations of the West, Lewis and Clark, Lieutenant Zebulon Pike and Major Stephen Long all recounted outcroppings of coal along the lower Missouri River. In the 1840s, Lieutenant John C. Frémont spotted plentiful outcroppings of coal along the North Platte River.

According to the U.S. Geological Survey's 1894 book *Geology of the Denver Basin*, the Sand Creek Mine, Township 4S, Range 65W—which is east of today's Aurora—is "said to have been the first discovery of coal in Colorado."

In 1859, coal was discovered in Marshall and the *Rocky Mountain News* reported coal and limestone discoveries "a few miles north of Denver City."

In the same year, Jim Baker, a former Indian scout who traveled with famous frontier scout Jim Bridger, settled for a few years on Coal Creek near what would become Erie. Baker was the first to "work" the area's coal and sold coal from exposed coal seams to his neighbors. He occasionally loaded his wagon with coal and traveled to Denver City, where eager buyers awaited.

Captain Ira Austin discovered the coal banks on the ridge east of downtown Erie in 1866 and sold eight hundred acres to the Boulder Valley Railroad Company, which proceeded to open the Boulder Valley Mine to fuel its locomotives. A few years later, the Star and Rob Roy mines opened in Canfield west of Erie.

In the early 1870s, Colorado Central Railroad executive C.C. Welch found the first coal in Louisville by accident. Welch hired a drilling rig to sink a well to supply water for the railroad crews working on the Denver-to-Cheyenne line, but the driller stumbled across a ten-foot vein of coal at two hundred feet. Welch sunk a shaft for the coal mine in 1877.

The first recorded evidence of coal near Lafayette was made in the summer of 1864 by General Land Office surveyor Hiram Witter, who noted in his field survey notebook for Township 1 South, Range 69 West that "in the NE 1/4 of the NE 1/4 of Sec. 1 is an outcrop of coal 1 chain long [66 feet] and 4 ft. thick, extent unknown." This would be the area where today's Baseline Road crosses over Coal Creek east of Lafayette. Witter drew a line through a notation in his notebook that the "coal bank had been opened" and replaced it with "coal outcrop." The notation "had been opened" may indicate that the coal was being "worked" by settlers.

Area pioneers gathered coal from surface outcrops to use for home heating. One outcropping of coal, mentioned by Mary Miller as being discovered in 1872, was located at about the center of the Foote-Miller Farm and mined by the Cambro/Pluto slope mine from 1917 to 1928.

Town founder Mary Miller and her brother James B. Foote leased some of their farmland north of the Cambro/Pluto coal outcrop first to John H. Simpson, who would sink two separate Lafayette coal mines—the Simpson in late 1887 and the Spencer in 1889—then to James Cannon Jr. in 1888. The Standard Mine, about one mile east of the Spencer-Simpson Mines, was also sunk in 1887.

WITH THE INVENTION OF the steam engine in the late 1700s, the Industrial Revolution was born. Coal used solely for heating homes began to be used in locomotives, in ocean liners and for specialized machinery in factories—all of which required coal to fire the steam boilers. This steam-powered revolution came west with the completion of the Transcontinental Railroad in 1869. Larger machines requiring larger steam power plants began arriving in Colorado by rail in 1873, and Denver's factories flourished.

By the early 1880s, railroads were the largest consumer of Colorado coal, and Lafayette joined the coal-mining bandwagon when Colorado & Southern Railway completed a three-mile spur from Louisville in 1889, paid for by the newly formed Spencer-Simpson Coal Company. That spur eventually connected to Erie. The railroad links to Erie, Louisville, Lafayette and Marshall coal mines nurtured the industrialization of coal mining—masses of men and machinery cranking out hundreds of tons of coal per day.

The coal under Lafayette and most of the area northwest of Denver known as the Northern Coal Field or Northern Field is sub-bituminous coal, a soft, friable coal that was highly suited for household heating stoves and for firing steam boilers. Sub-bituminous coal, also called lignite, had two problems when it came in contact with air, the first being that the coal could sometimes spontaneously combust. And miners discovered early on that coal burned just as efficiently underground as it did above ground. To avoid this,

Five men stand at a solid-rock formation inside the Vulcan coal mine in south Lafayette. Clarence A. "Gus" Waneka stands third from right. *Lafayette Public Library.*

Puritan coal mine east of Erie, 1922. The Puritan operated from 1908 to 1939 and employed coal miners from Erie, Brighton and Lafayette. *Lafayette Public Library*.

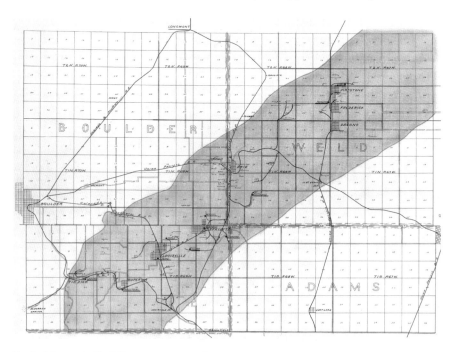

Rocky Mountain Fuel Company map of Northern Field holdings, 1920. *Denver Public Library, Western History Collection*.

at the end of the workday, the coal mines meticulously sealed airflow from a fresh coal face using brattice cloth. As the coal aged, it was less likely to spontaneously combust.

The second problem with sub-bituminous coal was that once it got to the surface, it started to degrade by absorbing moisture in the air. Left in the open air long enough, the coal became a soggy, unignitable black paste. This meant the coal couldn't be stored for a long period of time and was the reason it was mined in the winter months, when demand was higher. To solve the coal's short life span, some Dacono-area coal operators suggested building massive aboveground steel storage bins. From 1903 to 1904, area coal operators experimented with making coal briquettes, to no avail.

Thankfully, the railroad's quick-to-market system of hauling high volumes of recently mined coal to a nearby and voracious consumer market meant that the marginal coal didn't have to be stored and still retained exceptional value.

The Southern Coal Fields around Walsenburg and Trinidad produced a harder, coking coal that could be stored for long periods of time. The coking process heats coal to release impurities, and the resulting coke is pure carbon. Coke burns at higher temperatures and is used in blast furnaces to melt steel.

A significant factor in Lafayette's coal-mining history were the three successive Denver-based coal conglomerates—United Coal Company, Northern Coal Company and Rocky Mountain Fuel Company—that controlled coal production and employed thousands of local coal miners. From 1891, when United Coal was formed, to 1944, when Rocky Mountain Fuel reorganized and closed most of its mines, the coal operators influenced not only how mass-scale coal was mined, marketed and sold, but also how communities adjacent to the coal mines—Lafayette, Louisville, Erie, Canfield and Marshall—developed. The era of industrialized coal mining, defined by coal company executives in suits sitting around tables in downtown Denver offices, meant that some Boulder County towns survived and some didn't.

In 1898, only 5 percent of coal mined in Lafayette was used for home heating, the rest went to Denver power plants, manufacturers and steam locomotives. From June 1, 1897, to May 31, 1898, over 680,000 tons of coal were shipped to Denver from Northern Field coal mines. In the 1920s and 1930s, Great Western Sugar in Longmont and the Valmont Generating

Standard coal mine east of Lafayette on Blue Ribbon Hill, photographed in 1909 by Ed Tangen. *Lafayette Public Library.*

Remains of company housing along Coal Creek at the former Standard coal mine compound east of Lafayette, 2017. *Photograph by the author.*

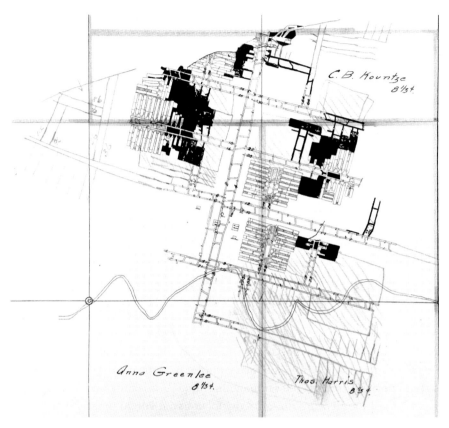

Vulcan coal mine progress map showing the mine's passageways, 1915. *Denver Public Library, Western History Collection.*

Station in Boulder were primary coal consumers. By the mid-1940s, most of the coal mines had closed.

If you live anywhere in the older parts of Lafayette, Louisville and Erie, it's likely that a coal mine removed most of the coal from the six- to twelve-foot seam hundreds of feet below ground. The mines were massive networks of passageways and rooms sometimes covering a square mile or more but almost always on one level. The passageways, called entries, were excavated as transportation corridors (also called haulageways). The rooms, where the coal was removed, could cover an area the size of a football field.

While little potential exists today of the ground above the mined areas collapsing or subsiding, there are modern examples of aboveground structures being damaged by subsidence. More often, though, subsidence is the result of a long neglected or inadequately sealed coal mine's vertical shafts.

BY THE LATE 1940s, the last coal-mining remnants at the site of the Simpson Mine included huge mounds of coal slack and broken shale pulled up from the depths over a period of four decades. The mounds of tailings also contained a large amount of red ash, a byproduct of the coal slack's spontaneous combustion.

Toward the center of the mostly flat but weed-infested thirty-eight-acre property was a fenced area marking the open mine shaft, about the top fifty feet still exposed to the elements but partially covered by a mixture of concrete and rebar. Frank Pankoski (1907–1983), who had purchased the Simpson Mine property (from Simpson Street south to Emma Street) for $900 in 1946, caved in the rest of the original Spencer shaft—renamed the Simpson shaft—using four dynamite charges, one at each corner of the fence.

In the early 1960s, the coal dump was portioned out to Frank A. "Shiny" Banyai, who used the tailings for fill under his newly built trailer court at East Cleveland Street and Burlington Avenue.

TYING UP LOOSE ENDS, in 1897, Mary Miller filed an affidavit with the Boulder County Clerk and Recorder stating that her 1881 Foote-Miller Farm coal lease with Walter H. Underwood was null and void because Underwood had "disappeared." The 1881 coal lease "required the said Walter H. Underwood, within 90 days, to commence exploring for coal on said land, yet the said Underwood never did any work of any kind," stated the affidavit. "The said Underwood was a stranger to the affiant, but obtained the said lease by representing that he would immediately explore the said land for coal and open a coal mine thereon, but that shortly after the said lease had been executed and delivered to him the said Underwood went away and never returned."

James B. Foote, who'd secured lucrative coal contracts with both the Simpsons and James Cannon Jr., moved to Boulder and became a prominent politician, but he lost his wealth in bad investments (including a failed liquor distributorship) and died a poor man in 1895. John H. Simpson, the ambitious coal prospector, mining engineer and entrepreneur who helped put Lafayette and Louisville on the map, died nearly penniless in 1909.

During the thirty-year Miller/Foote leases, from 1889 to 1919, the Spencer-Simpson Mine produced 3,999,771 tons of coal, of which about 50 percent would have been lump coal. At 12.5¢ per ton of lump coal, royalties paid to Mary Miller totaled about $250,000—at least $3.9 million when translated into 2020 dollars.

New Centennial coal mine operated south of Lafayette from 1936 to 1952. Photographed in 1946 by Russell Lee. *Department of Interior, Solid Fuels Administration for War.*

Mine tailings (slag heap) remaining from the Centennial coal mine, located west of Cherrywood Drive in Lafayette, 2020. *Photograph by the author.*

LAFAYETTE COAL MINES

Big Lake/Garibaldi. Main shaft lies south of Baseline Road and west of Waneka Lake. Thickness of seams: unknown; year of operation: 1916; coal produced: 3,449 tons; number of employees: unknown.

Black Diamond. Located at the northwest corner of Highway 287 and Baseline Road. Main level depth: 268 feet; thickness of seams: 4 feet, 6 inches to 6 feet; years of operation: 1931–56; peak production year: 1932 (58,385 tons); coal produced: 801,657 tons; number of employees: 62.

Cannon. Main shaft was a few feet south of today's East Emma Street and adjacent to Merlin Drive. Cannon Mine was sunk by the Cannon family but closed in 1898 because the soft brick lining of the main shaft collapsed. A typo in the record-keeping ledgers at the Colorado Division of Reclamation, Mining and Safety shows the mine as the "CANON." In later years of production, the mine was referred to as the Otis Mine. Main level depth: 210 feet; thickness of seam: 8 feet to 14 feet; years of operation: 1888–98; peak production year: 1890 (61,771 tons); coal produced: 130,017 tons; number of employees: 32 (1898).

Capitol. Main shaft lies east of 119th Street and west of Coal Creek along the south side of Flagg Drive (before it turns north). Main level depth: 212 feet; thickness of seams: 5 feet, 8 inches; years of operation: 1907–25; peak production year: 1909 (93,228 tons); coal produced: 515,092 tons; number of employees: 86 (1911).

Centennial (New). Located between today's Empire Road and South Cherrywood Drive in the southwest corner of Lafayette. Main level depth: 285 feet; thickness of seam: 5 feet, 6 inches; years of operation: 1936–52; peak production year: 1942 (201,073 tons); coal produced: 1,834,763 tons; number of employees: 323 (1939).

Columbine. Located about four miles northeast of Lafayette, now the Erie landfill. Main level depth: 300 feet; thickness of seams: 6 feet to 12 feet; years of operation: 1905; 1920–1946; Peak production year: 1922, 409,836 tons; coal produced: 7,216,286 tons; No. employees: 239 (1937).

Electric/Summit. Located southeast of Waneka Lake and adjacent to the coal-fueled power plant. Main level depth: 206 feet; thickness of seams: 5 feet, 6 inches; years of operation: 1898–1918; peak production year: 1908 (37,600 tons); coal produced: 73,839 tons; number of employees: 27 (1912).

Excelsior. Main shaft lies north of Brooks Avenue at Baseline Road and south of Arapahoe Road. Main level depth: unknown; thickness of seam: 14 feet, 8 inches; years of operation: 1890–1913; peak production year: 1893 (105,000 tons); coal produced: 487,584 tons; number of employees: 65.

Gladstone. Located north of Brooks Avenue at Baseline Road and south of Arapahoe Road. Main level depth: 240 feet; thickness of seam: 14 feet; years of operation: 1890–1916; peak production year: 1897 (52,214 tons); coal produced: 427,878 tons; number of employees: 40.

Hi-Way. Located southeast of Lafayette. The main shaft was along Dillon Road just east of Highway 287. Main level depth: 385 feet; thickness of seams: 6 feet to 7 feet; years of operation: 1930–54; peak production year: 1942 (161,646 tons); coal produced: 2,333,939 tons; number of employees: 138.

Mitchell. Located north of Brooks Avenue at Baseline Road and south of Arapahoe Road. The Mitchells also operated a "Mitchell Mine" in Canfield during the 1870s. Main level depth: 220 feet; thickness of seam: 7 feet to 14 feet; years of operation: 1893–1920; peak production year: 1917 (102,175 tons); coal produced: 1,295,229 tons; number of employees: 81.

Senator. Owned by the Willoughby Coal and Land Company and located southeast of Old Town Lafayette. Richard Morgan and William Padfield bought and moved the tipple and hoisting equipment from the Gladstone Mine, which closed in 1905. Main level depth: 116 feet; thickness of seams: 7 feet, 7 inches; years of operation: 1906–13; peak production year: 1938 (58,385 tons); coal produced: 801,657 tons; number of employees: 13 (1911).

Spencer-Simpson. Commonly known as the Simpson Mine, located under most of Old Town Lafayette, extending from Lucerne Drive at its northern boundary to both East and West Emma Street on its southern boundary. Two different shafts and tipples serviced what at one time were two separate mines. The mines combined in 1893 under the name "Simpson." The main shaft and tipple for the Spencer, located in the 700 block of East Cleveland

Street, served the combined mine. The Simpson no. 2 shaft, sunk in 1887, was located in the alley of the 800 block of East Simpson Street but was used as an air shaft after a fire destroyed the tipple and engine house over the shaft on November 13, 1897. A later report by the Colorado Inspector of Coal Mines said that the fire originated by "tramps lighting a fire in the old building." Coal lease holders as of 1909: Mary Miller and Harriet Foote, each receiving twelve and a half cents per ton of lump coal only. Main level depth: 243 feet; thickness of seam: 6 feet, 0 inches to 14 feet, 0 inches; years of operation: 1888–1926; peak production year: 1906 (220,529 tons); coal produced: 4,738,248 tons; number of employees: 115.

Standard. Located east of Old Town Lafayette near Blue Ribbon Hill, the Standard Mine lies under Coal Creek and Rock Creek from roughly Baseline Road on the north to the Northwest Parkway on the south. The main shaft and tipple were located about three hundred yards southeast of Flagg Park Trailhead along the Coal Creek trail. Upper level depth: 261 feet; lower level depth: 320 feet; thickness of seams: 5 feet, 6 inches to 8 feet, 0 inches; years of operation: 1888–93; 1905–37; peak production year: 1909 (190,668 tons); coal produced: 2,291,603 tons; number of employees: 200 (1908).

Storrs. Located north of the Capitol Mine, along Highway 7 just west of County Line Road. Main level depth: unknown; thickness of seams: 5 feet; years of operation: 1898–1900; peak production year: 1900 (18,100 tons); coal produced: 29,529 tons; number of employees: unknown.

Strathmore. Opened in 1901 by Mary Miller's oldest son, Thomas, the Strathmore Mine lies roughly south of East Emma Street and north of South Boulder Road. The main shaft and tipple were located at today's Skylark Drive and Skylark Circle. Thomas Miller was decapitated in an accident at the mine on January 28, 1902. The Strathmore is similar to the Standard Mine in that coal was mined on multiple levels. Early mining extracted the topmost layer, which was shallow, about 50 to 75 feet. Later mining involved tunneling downward to another level to extract the second vein of coal, at about 180 feet. Mining overlapping coal seams increased the chance of subsidence events filtering through to the surface. Main level depth: 25 to 75 feet; lower level depth: 180 feet; thickness of seams: 8 feet, 0 inches to 12 feet, 0 inches; years of operation: 1901–19; peak production year: 1906 (43,920 tons); coal produced: 439,433 tons; number of employees: 39.

Vaughn. A slope entry mine located north of the Standard Mine on Blue Ribbon Hill east of Lafayette. Main level depth: unknown; thickness of seams: 13 feet, 6 inches; years of operation: 1897–1906; peak production year: 1901 (10,653 tons); coal produced: 44,167 tons; number of employees: unknown.

Vulcan. Sunk in 1903 and located south of South Boulder Road and north of and under Coal Creek. Coal lease holders in 1909 receiving eight-and-one-third-cent royalty per ton: William Harmon, Anna Waneka Greenlee and Thomas Harris. Main level depth: 182 feet; thickness of seam: 49 inches to 62 inches; years of operation: 1903–37; peak production year: 1920 (96,914 tons); coal produced: 1,497,049 tons; number of employees: 73.

5

THE LIQUOR CLAUSE

Founder Mary Miller platted Lafayette as a dry town. Her temperance beliefs were formed after her husband's battle with alcoholism.

A prosperous town is Lafayette,
More so than those around,
Because so much of mineral wealth
Lies buried in the ground.
There's no saloon in all the town
Where men can liquor get.
'Tis banished, and forever, too,
From pleasant Lafayette.
—Greeley Tribune, May 26, 1892

Though not publicly acknowledged, Mary Miller's husband, Lafayette, likely died from complications caused by overconsumption of alcohol, which transformed his widow (and former saloon co-owner) into a prohibitionist, a member of a national movement to outlaw production, distribution and consumption of alcohol.

Town lots that Mary Miller sold starting in 1888 as part of her original Lafayette plat, the area of Old Town east of Public Road, included "The Alcohol Cause," a deed restriction stating, "no spiritous, vinous or malt liquors shall ever be sold or given away as a beverage, on the premises, under penalty of forfeiting all rights, title and interest" in the property. Old Town

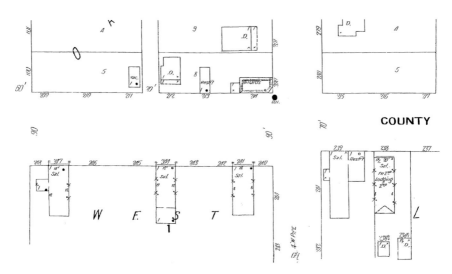

View of four of Lafayette's five saloons along the west side of Public Road. *Sanborn Fire Insurance Map, 1908. Public domain.*

property owners could acquire and consume alcohol on their deed-restricted lots, just not give away or sell it.

Naturally, this meant that no saloons could occupy any lot.

Lafayette town board minutes from December 1, 1890, show that the town's first recorded saloon license was "granted to Anthony Oats for the purpose of carrying on the saloon business in Lafayette—formerly known as East Louisville." This would have been the area known as "Saloon Row" on the west side of Public Road and north of Simpson Street.

The front page of the June 21, 1892 *Boulder Daily Camera* carried news of a large fire in Lafayette that destroyed one of four saloons along the west side of Public Road. The North Star saloon, owned by Jerry Arnold of the Boulder City Brewing Company, was a complete loss. A related news item revealed that some residents were glad to see the saloon burn. The report said that Lafayette's anti-saloon Good Templars "now number over 60, with three saloons and one now smoldering in ashes."

Arnold announced that he would rebuild in September 1892, and the pro-saloon *Boulder Daily Camera* reported that "Lafayette is to revel in the glories of a new saloon to rise in the ruins of Jerry Arnold's old place, recently destroyed by fire." A saloon that Arnold owned in Lyons burned on September 6, 1892, and Arnold's rebuilt Lafayette saloon burned to the ground again in February 1893.

The Lafayette Good Templars prohibition group was an offshoot of the national organization, the Independent Order of Good Templars, founded in Utica, New York, in 1851. Mary Miller was a member of the local group and probably helped launch it. A few years later, Miller formed the Lafayette Law and Order League, whose mission was to close saloons operating in the town of Lafayette. She was also a member of the Woman's Christian Temperance Union and was a regular attendee at the Boulder chapter, founded in 1881. Her early and closest allies in efforts to keep saloons out of Lafayette were George Cannon, James Cannon Jr. and John H. Simpson, who prospected coal and obtained mineral rights from Mary Miller to sink the Spencer and Simpson Mines.

Mary Miller was affiliated with the Prohibition Party of Colorado since its inception. It was formerly the state Temperance Union, which was formed in Denver in 1884. The national party's platform included the "prohibition of importation, exportation, manufacture and sale of all alcoholic and intoxicating liquors" and demanded "scientific instruction in our public schools concerning the effect of alcohol, nicotine and narcotic poisons upon the human organization." The Prohibition Party's symbol was a camel.

As a Congregationalist (and not a Methodist), Mary Miller's prohibitionist beliefs were rooted in her husband's battle with alcohol addiction, which probably started when the Millers and Mary's brother James B. Foote ran their Miller Tavern Ranch saloon and stage stop starting in 1866. There is evidence that Lafe Miller literally consumed all of the profits.

Thomas J. Lindsey owned the Rock Creek House starting in 1864 and sold it to the Millers and Foote in the spring 1866, at which time the food and drinking establishment's name was changed to Miller Tavern. The Millers had moved to Rock Creek the year before.

Lindsey appeared with Lafe before the Boulder County Commissioners on July 3, 1866, and meeting minutes state that "D.L. Miller and Lindsey presented bond and made application for a license to keep a Saloon at the Rock Creek House from the First day of May 1866 until the first day of October 1866." (DeLafayette's name was abbreviated in many Boulder County records as "D.L.") At the time, a county saloon license required a $500 bond and a $50 annual renewal fee.

Dipped from a ten-gallon barrel of whiskey likely obtained from Bernard Slavin's Wholesale Liquor Emporium in West Denver, a one-and-a-half-ounce shot of Old Kentucky Bourbon was sold by the Millers for the prevailing rate of twelve and a half cents.

By 1869, there were signs that the Rock Creek enterprise was in financial trouble. "Miller and Foote" were listed in Boulder County's 1868 delinquent tax list, owing just under $70 in back taxes. In 1872, Thomas J. Lindsey filed a lawsuit in Boulder District Court alleging that James B. Foote reneged on the ranchland and tavern purchase and failed to repay a one-year promissory note, dated July 16, 1866, for $1,000. Lindsey demanded another $4,000 for unpaid "goods, wares and merchandise."

Coincidental with the lawsuit, the Millers and Foote sold the Miller Tavern Ranch to Abner C. Goodhue. In July 1872, Foote was ordered by the court to pay Lindsey $1,654 plus court costs.

In late 1871, the Millers moved to Erie, where Lafe opened a meat market. In 1874, they moved to Boulder. Lafe opened a downtown butcher shop selling beef sourced from ranches in Elbert County. Shortly thereafter, Lafe got back into the liquor business. The May 17, 1877 edition of the *Colorado Banner* reported: "Lafe Miller is putting up a brick [structure] east of butcher shop. It will be occupied by a wholesale liquor establishment." Later *Banner* editions regularly chronicle Lafe Miller as being "under the weather due to rheumatism."

Lafe Miller died in May 1878 at age thirty-eight. News accounts listed the cause of death as everything from a "bowel obstruction" to "congestion of the bowels" (derived from an archaic medical term known as "Coeliaemia" and defined as the congestion of the blood vessels of the abdomen) to "an acute attack of Bright's disease of the kidneys, coupled with a derangement of the liver."

Even though Mary Miller's deed restrictions limited the sale of alcohol, saloons on the west side of Public Road were thriving. In 1905, the *Lafayette Leader* reported that seven saloons were doing business on the west side of Public Road. A saloon license was $500 to $700, or about $14,000 to $20,000 in 2020 dollars.

Mary Miller's alcohol deed restrictions on properties east of Public Road controlled the distribution of alcohol, but not its consumption. A typical after-work routine was for miners to send their kids up the hill to the saloons with a wood pail to retrieve beer. Frank Miller said in 1968 that "practically every coal miner in the town would send his son or his daughter up to the saloon" to get beer to cart home. Delbert Reddington (1916–2008) said that the insides of the wood buckets were greased to prevent leaking and to keep the beer from foaming too much.

IN MARCH 1902, MARY Miller penned an open letter to the prohibitionist *Lafayette News* asking the town trustees to act on a petition signed by three hundred residents demanding that saloons be closed because the drunk and disorderly clientele were creating disturbances. Mary accused the board of mishandling the petition, which somehow made its way to public display at Peter M. Peltier's Elkhorn Saloon, a Public Road drinking house. Peltier was part owner of the Centennial Mine near Louisville and the State Mine near Erie. "I demand to know who is responsible for this insult to the [Lafayette Law and Order] League, and to the three hundred citizens who signed the petition," Miller wrote.

A nationwide organization, the Law and Order League's primary tenet was the prohibition of alcohol. The organization's constitution stated that "the enforcement of law is essential to the perpetuity of good government." League chapters in southern U.S. cities actively opposed lynchings, but available records show that the Lafayette chapter concentrated on the virtues of temperance.

In 1905, pro-saloon *Lafayette Leader* editor Jack DeMotte took an unpopular stance on the saloon question. His March 8, 1905 editorial favored affordable Boulder County licensing fees for the saloons. "The population of Lafayette is made up to a considerable degree of foreigners," wrote DeMotte. "The use of intoxicants is a part of their lives. Law cannot change their habits. If saloons are driven out, they will be supplied by the bootlegger or the divekeeper. More than likely, on each pay night, they will go to Denver, there to remain until their money is gone. If he cannot satisfy his appetite, in the open saloon, he will do so elsewhere."

An attempt by Mary Miller to enforce the alcohol deed restriction for properties east of Public Road was publicized in October 1911, the second year of the Long Strike that polarized the town. An explosion damaged a tin shed behind the Bermont & Van DeBergh mercantile store (the Abner C. Goodhue Building), located a block northwest of Miller's home at East Cleveland and Michigan. Someone had snuck into the shed behind the mercantile and ignited a "small quantity of an explosive," according to the *Lafayette Leader*.

Mary Miller, who demanded forfeiture of the lot and building in a filing with the county clerk, suspected that the explosion was related to the drunken renters of the second floor of the mercantile, the Citizens' Alliance Social Club. Because Lafayette's saloons on the west side of Public Road were frequented by the striking union men, nonunion workers and guards from the mine gathered regularly at private social clubs on the east side.

East Simpson Street, looking west, circa 1909. *Author's collection.*

Sarah Kettle stands behind the counter in her fabric and notions store at 208 East Simpson. Ribbons and buttons are in cases, and bolts of fabric sit on shelves. *Lafayette Miners Museum.*

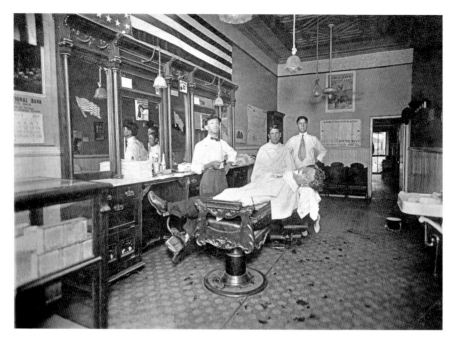

East Simpson barber shop, 1917. *Lafayette Miners Museum.*

The building's owners, George Bermont and Jay O. Van DeBergh, were former business partners of Mary Miller's. In 1905, the investment group funded the construction of the flour mill located on Baseline Road. In her 1911 attempted repossession of the Bermont/Van DeBergh property, Bermont and Van DeBergh accused Miller of "attempting to aid the union cause without showing any justice or mercy."

THE REPEAL OF THE Eighteenth Amendment prohibiting the manufacture, sale or consumption alcohol, known as Prohibition, was finalized on December 5, 1933. Less than a month later, the first retail liquor store in Boulder County opened in—you guessed it—Lafayette. It was located on "the main highway," now Public Road. The owner, T.C. Meyer, paid $300 for the Lafayette license.

6

NOTABLE PLACES LOST AND FOUND

Lafayette's early "Main Street" on East Simpson Street was once a bustling center of commerce that featured blacksmiths, jewelers, banks, retailers, grocery stores and a movie theater. It included the Lafayette Bank and the Goodhue Building.

The December 18, 1914 front-page story in the *Lafayette Leader* about the failure of Lafayette Bank and Trust Company didn't explain a whole lot about the circumstances behind the bank's sudden closing, only that the bank had been consolidated with the Louisville Bank and Trust Company. "The public is to be congratulated on the consolidation strength thus attained which will show the aggregated resources to be over $350,000," said the story.

A month later, the story got worse. On January 16, 1915, the newspaper reported that Louisville Bank and Trust Company was insolvent and had been turned over to the State Banking Department "pending the suit in regard to the account of the United Mine Workers which is now in litigation."

That was that, at least according to the local press.

Using coal royalties and land sales proceeds, Mary Miller founded the Farmers' & Miners' State Bank in 1892 with S.T. Hooper, C.C. Brown and G.C. Beaman. It closed in 1894. She then opened Lafayette Bank and Trust Company, also known as the Miller Bank, in 1900.

The 400 block of East Simpson Street, including the Rocky Mountain Company Store building (*left*) and the Lafayette Bank building. *Lafayette Public Library.*

Her second bank, Lafayette Bank, provided many "firsts" for the U.S. banking industry, including Miller as the first female president of a bank. That fact came to light from a news article printed in the December 12, 1902 *Lafayette News*, reprinted from a Denver daily newspaper. The scope of Miller's banking acumen has been inflated locally in the decades since, to the point that she was labeled the first female bank president in the "whole world." While it's possible, there's no evidence of it.

Mary Miller frequently extended mortgages to women to help them build credit worthiness, and most of the town's coal miners were secure in their own homes—not paying rent or living in company housing—thanks to her. During the frequent strikes, she allowed union miners to delay their mortgage payments.

There are several versions of the 1914 bank failure. James P. Miller, Mary's son and vice-president of the bank in 1914, claimed that political pressure as a result of the bank's support of the striking miners caused a "great shock" that the bank couldn't recover from.

Ralph Clinton Miller, Mary's great-grandson, said in 1988 that Mary's son James "took the money from the bank. The bank went broke and they seem to think he took the money and went to Texas and never came back."

Frank Miller, Mary Miller's grandson, said in 1978 that the bank failure was caused by a delinquent reimbursement of $5 per family per week strike subsidies, known as a selective strike fund, paid by the union to striking miners. The United Mine Workers of America told the bank to accept miners' drafts, which the bank did, but the $90,000 the bank was supposed to send for reimbursement never made it west from the United Mine Workers of America central office in Indianapolis.

In July 1916, a local news article stated that $80,000 deposited with the Lafayette bank, then in receivership, was released to depositors, including the UMWA, over the objection of bank officer James P. Miller. The UMWA said that the money was deposited at the bank with the understanding that it would be loaned to the American Fuel Company to pay wages of union miners trying to break the strike.

NEWSPAPER REPORTS OF TURN-OF-THE-CENTURY subsidence events are sparse, but the lawsuit surrounding subsidence at the Abner C. Goodhue (Bermont) building was well reported.

In the summer of 1902, a sinkhole next to the A.C. Goodhue Building at 311 East Simpson Street (Block E, Lot 12) was reported "filled up and leveled" in the *Lafayette News*, which "contributed to the improvement and appearance of the street."

East Simpson Street, looking west in 1907, including the Goodhue Building that housed the Bermont & Van DeBergh mercantile. *Author's collection.*

The building was erected for $8,000 in 1892 by W.O. Van Etten for George B. Cannon, but it was purchased by Abner C. Goodhue in 1893 and housed the Cannon & Bermont general store, followed by the George E. Bermont Dry Goods and Groceries store. W.D. Cannon, brother of George Cannon and James Cannon Jr., was Bermont's early partner.

Goodhue initiated a lawsuit against Northern Coal and Coke Company, owner of the Simpson Mine, in 1903. Goodhue claimed that undermining had caused the damage. He asked for damages of $19,000.

Photos taken for the jury trial in 1903 by Boulder photographer J.B. Sturtevant show the second story on the south side of the brick building leaning a few degrees toward the street.

In December 1903, a Boulder jury agreed with the subsidence claim and awarded Goodhue $3,650.

The (leaning) second floor of the A.C. Goodhue Building was not removed until the 1940s. The building later housed a grocery store and was torn down about 1999.

THE LATE WINTER OF 1896 was a tough one for teachers and students at the two-story brick school located at Baseline Road and Iowa Avenue in Lafayette, known as the first Baseline School.

An early February 1896 front-page write-up in the *Boulder Daily Camera* detailed the extramarital affair of two "school officials," likely principal G.L. Dillworth and teacher Ella Walton, who had been "caught in a lascivious affair after school hours that was, to say the least, unduly intimate."

"The liaison is the subject of considerable excitement in the coal camp and may lead to divorce and proceedings for adultery," said the *Daily Camera* story.

Elizabeth C. Barnd, who taught the school's elementary-age pupils alongside her sister Ruth A. Barnd, spent that February trying to keep her fifty-eight students focused on schoolwork. Quelling students' speculation related to the tryst muttered during grammar lessons was but one of her concerns.

The other was the cold winter wind making its way through the cracks and crevices of the exterior walls of her first-floor classroom. Some of the one-half-inch-wide vertical cracks in the brick could be stuffed with newspapers to stop the draft. But on cold winter days, the coal stove in the corner of the classroom didn't offer much help, and her students often sat at their desks in their winter coats. On windy days, the draft through the wall cracks was so significant that smoke exiting the coal stove's rooftop stovepipe was drawn back into the classrooms. When the wind was strong, classes were excused from school because the building shook so badly. Teachers were cautious for a reason: Seven years earlier, newspapers reported that on January 24, 1890, strong winds blew down one of the brick walls "of the fine new school."

The school building was erected about 1889 using soft bricks from the local Dutch Colony brickworks. By 1894, prominent cracks from foundation to roof started forming. Although the Simpson Mine had removed coal two hundred feet below the school, no one gave a second thought that the mine might be causing the damage. The bricks were bad—and that was that.

In 1904, RESIDENTS FUNDED the building of a new wood frame school on Baseline Road, built on the same footprint as the old brick school. The $10,000 construction cost included a "substantial" stone foundation and plentiful windows to let in natural light.

The Baseline School, a two-story wood structure, at Iowa Avenue and East Baseline Road, circa 1908. *Lafayette Public Library*.

The abandoned Baseline School was destroyed by fire in 1964. *Waneka family collection.*

Over a decade later, in the first week of May 1917, Denver newspapers stated that J. Mitchell, Colorado state inspector of factories, had inspected the wood frame schoolhouse on Baseline, found that it was structurally unsound due to subsidence caused by coal mining and ordered the building vacated. On May 11, town residents met at the condemned building and agreed to close the school and send the schoolchildren to classes at Union Hall, located at Simpson Street and Gough Avenue. Some in the crowd blamed the problem on the architect rather than the coal company.

At the opening of the school year the next October, several buildings in town had been retrofitted for classrooms. High school students were sent to the Baptist Church on West Simpson Street, and the primary grades attended classes in the basement of the Methodist church at Gough Avenue and Geneseo Street. Third and sixth grades occupied a vacant saloon, the Coors and Zang on Public Road, which had been closed in 1915 because of a statewide vote to make Colorado a dry state.

During the 1917 summer break, the Rocky Mountain Fuel Company (RM Fuel)—owners of the Simpson Mine—gave school board member Thomas Knill a tour of the subterranean mine passageways under the wood frame Baseline School. On August 23, RM Fuel's chief engineer, Harry M. Jones, took Knill to entries directly under the new Baseline School. Jones was based in Denver but got his start as engineer at the Simpson Mine, so he knew every nook and cranny.

"We were able to make an examination on #35 and #37 entries as far west as the cross-cut located 95 feet west of room #9 off #37 entry, same being almost directly under the front of the school building," wrote Jones in a letter to the board. "At this point the roof had caved in both #35 and #37 entries which undoubtedly resulted from the workings taking only the top bench of coal and not enough roof coal left to support the weak roof for the number of years it has been standing. The coal being worked in this place is from 6 1/2 to 7 feet in thickness. We found the coal directly under the reserve left to support the school building is still in place and that our map represents the actual conditions as they now, and for years past, have existed, in this particular district."

Jones didn't mention that the area under the school had been mined in the early 1890s.

In November 1917, the Lafayette School Board sent Louisville attorney Ed Affolter to Boulder District Court to recover damages for the sagging school structure. Affolter asked for $35,000 in damages against the Union Pacific Railroad, Northern Coal and Coke Company and Rocky Mountain Fuel Company. The lawsuit stated that the companies owned the coal land under the school between 1900 and 1911 and "failed to take proper precautions against subsidence of the ground."

In May 1918, the lawsuit was dismissed. By early June, the school board had already slated a June 28 bond issue election to raise $15,000 to repair the school. Architects promised an addition to the school that would include a new heating plant and an assembly hall. The *Lafayette Leader* advocated for the property tax increase by running an architect's rendering of the remodeled school. The drawing shows a building almost four times larger than the damaged school. "The present second floor and tower will be removed and the general effect of combined buildings will present a quiet bungalow effect that will be most pleasing to the most critical," said the *Leader* story. Property owners passed the bond issue by a vote of sixty-one to thirty-four.

A Boulder contractor quickly began repairing the building, which was lifted in the air and placed on a new foundation, and the walls were reinforced with steel girders. The north wing of the building was torn down and rebuilt. By late summer, repair costs overwhelmed the school district's budget, forcing another bond issue, this time for $10,000. The second bond issue passed by a vote of thirteen to three. The remodeled

Baseline School, coming in over budget and with only a slightly larger footprint, reopened in December 1918.

When the Rocky Mountain Fuel Company purchased Northern Coal and Coke Company in 1911, the company inherited the Simpson Mine, a flagship coal mine that was feeling its age. Most of the coal inside the twenty-two-year-old mine's one-and-a-half-square-mile footprint had been removed. What was left, called the "easy coal," included the coal support pillars, also called stumps, that lined the haulageways and entries. As was the case in all Boulder County coal mines, the pillars kept the rock ceiling of the haulageways from collapsing. With the rest of the coal within the mine's boundaries nearly exhausted, RM Fuel made a decision to grab "the good stuff." The easy coal left in the Simpson Mine was profitable, but removing the last subterranean coal supports led to tunnel collapse in almost all cases and often resulted in sinking soil on the surface.

From 1911 to 1920, dozens of Lafayette homeowners sought relief from Rocky Mountain Fuel Company for homes that were shifting and sinking from mine subsidence. Some residential lots had sunk five feet. In 1914, soil settled around the city's main water pipeline on Baseline Road from the cemetery east to Public Road, as did the soil around structures along the 100 and 200 blocks of West Baseline. Lafayette mayor and store owner Thomas Faull spent most of the summer of 1914 exchanging letters with RM Fuel, imploring it to repair the damaged roadway and pipeline. This was the second subsidence confrontation the town initiated with the owners of the Simpson Mine. In March 1901, the town threatened a $20,000 lawsuit if the Northern Coal and Coke Company didn't fix sinking streets alleged to have been caused by the mine. Town trustee minutes from April state that "said company has agreed to grade and put in level condition the streets and alleys that are affected on the corner of Iowa and Simpson streets and also the sinking about the city jail [at Simpson and Harrison] and the Colorado & Southern Railroad Company's depot [on Finch Avenue near Cannon Street]."

In the 1910s and 1920s, stacks of correspondence between RM Fuel attorneys and distraught homeowners and their lawyers showed that the west side of Public Road was hardest hit by subsidence. West Simpson and Cleveland Streets tallied eight homes damaged and an entire block of West Emma sank.

East of Public Road, Mary Jane "Polly" (Simpson) Morgan's house at 211 East Cannon showed signs of settling. Polly was the daughter of Joseph Simpson, who was the brother of John H. Simpson. Her sisters were Rose

Simpson and Ena (Simpson) Jones. Polly married State Senator Richard W. Morgan in 1901. RM Fuel said that no coal had been mined under Polly's house since 1903 but agreed to settle out of court in 1914 for $200. Residents of the 200 block of East Emma—C.E. Wilkinson, George Nace and his brother Lewis—settled out of court for $350 each. Several houses north of Nace's and up the hill toward Simpson and Cleveland Streets were severely damaged by subsidence and were abandoned by the residents.

The bulk of the residential lots in the "newer" subdivisions that came after Mary Miller's 1888–89 town platting, including Hopkin's, Mountain View, Excelsior Place, First Union and Industrial City, had deed attachments advising buyers of limited liability for anything related to coal extraction. The Union Pacific Railroad and the Northern Coal and Coke Company made it clear in writing that buyers of the land accepted full responsibility for any shifting of soil or subsidence that resulted from coal that was removed from under the property.

But RM Fuel could be held accountable if the subsidence was a result of recent mining—any mining that commenced after the date it had purchased Northern Coal and Coke, October 11, 1911.

RM Fuel settlement records show that the company stepped up and paid damage claims for areas where it had pulled pillars. In some subsidence cases, the company refused to pay. In 1921, Baseline Road resident J. Mary Burt sued RM Fuel for damage to her home due to subsidence. Her home, three blocks east of the Baseline School, had been built prior to 1907. In the lawsuit, RM Fuel claimed it hadn't mined coal within eight hundred feet of Burt's home and that any damage caused by subsidence would occur within thirty days of the pillars being removed. A lower court dismissed Burt's lawsuit, but the Colorado Supreme Court intervened and said that "the plaintiff's [Burt's] lot and other land adjacent and near it sank, that there was, at some point in time or other, mining, followed by pulling of stumps and other supports, very nearly under the lot. Land does not sink without cause, and but one possible cause appears."

Very little evidence of Lafayette's coal-mining past remains today. A few structures moved from the mine camps dot Old Town, and the Lafayette Miner's Museum retains some of the tools of the coal-mining trade.

Below the surface, voids where coal was removed still remain and filter through to the surface from time to time. Over 7,100 acres in Boulder County are designated by the U.S. Geological Survey as subsidence hazard zones, with 1,014 total in Lafayette. About 285 of those acres are categorized as moderate to high hazards. Until 1975, only forty-one cases of subsidence were reported.

According to the 1911–12 Colorado Coal Inspector's Report, the Simpson Mine started replacing timber supports in main haulageways with "concrete and stone stopping." Timber supports would degrade and collapse after a few decades. Passageways supported by stone and concrete may not collapse for hundreds of years.

Test drilling done in 1973 indicated that less than 10 percent of the mined area under Lafayette still had voids or open areas. David Holm with the Inactive Mine Reclamation program of the Colorado Mined Land Reclamation Division stated at the time that "still presenting a serious hazard to humans were dozens of vertical shafts that appear to be closed but are simply filled with plugs of dirt and debris, which could give way at any time."

On July 17, 1979, the airshaft for the Spencer-Simpson Mine, formerly the Simpson no. 2 main shaft, collapsed in the backyard of Warren Krueger's house at 802 East Simpson in Lafayette. The area of subsidence was sixteen feet wide and five feet deep and was confirmed to be a part of the former Spencer-Simpson Mine by mining engineer Louis Gaz. Called the "Krueger-Mulock cave-in," the event caused little damage to structures. In the months that followed, a five- to eight-foot concrete plug was poured to seal the shaft.

Gaz also verified the collapse of the Spencer shaft, about two hundred yards southwest of the Simpson no. 2 shaft, in the early 1960s in the middle of the street in the 700 block of East Cleveland. A concrete truck en route to "Shiny" Banyai's trailer court on East Cleveland punched through the cap for the shaft. The "Spencer shaft" was renamed the "Simpson shaft" in about 1898.

The same shaft collapsed again in 2015, nearly swallowing an SUV and its driver. In 2016, the Colorado Division of Reclamation, Mining and Safety poured a two-hundred-foot column of concrete that filled and permanently sealed the abandoned mine shaft.

7

ANCIENT TRAILS AND STEEL RAILS

Centuries-old transportation corridors bisected Lafayette, and the Overland Stage Coach brought people and mail to a growing frontier.

ARCHAEOLOGICAL EVIDENCE OF THE Lafayette area's first inhabitants, uncovered in 1990 and 1993 on the banks of Rock Creek at what is known today as Rock Creek Farm—land that Mary Miller's brother James B. Foote patented in 1870 and where DeLafayette and Mary Miller operated a stagecoach stop—included an aboriginal campsite dating from 6000 BC and AD 1500. Pottery sherds, projectile points, burned seeds, charred animal bone and bone tools recovered from the site date to the Ceramic Period, five hundred to two thousand years ago, and showed multiple occupations of the site between AD 850 and 1300. Analysis of the bone fragments around the firepit showed that the inhabitants' diet consisted mostly of prairie dog and rabbit.

In research published in 1942, archaeologist Ronald L. Ives detailed the remnants of a series of long-established hunting camps extending for miles along the banks of Coal Creek near Marshall. Investigations disclosed tepee circles, fireplaces, artifacts and "buffalo bones in quantity."

Other indications of early inhabitants of our area include ancient petroglyphs, tools and arrow points at White Rock (next to Boulder Creek at Ninety-Fifth Street northwest of Lafayette) and long faded single-track trails next to nearly every east–west stream corridor in east Boulder County.

Tracing of an ancient petroglyph at White Rock, northwest of Lafayette. *From the report "Graphics and Incised Inscriptions on the White Rocks, Boulder County" prepared for the City of Boulder Open Space Department by Jean Matthews Kindig and Indian Peaks Chapter of the Colorado Archaeological Society, 1998.*

According to longtime Lafayette resident Charles "Chuck" Waneka, whose ancestor Adolf Waneka homesteaded near Lafayette starting in 1861, most Front Range streams had a trail that was made by Native Americans.

Ives also described in 1942 an ancient high-country Indian trail system over Arapaho Pass, down Middle Boulder Creek through Nederland, Boulder, Valmont and terminating at White Rock east of Boulder. Another trail from Nederland along South Boulder Creek and through Eldorado Gap "joined an ancient trail connecting the Coal Creek [near Eldorado Springs] and Boulder camps."

Foothills-to-flatland trail systems were considered sacred and were used by Native Americans for millennia—they camped at the base of the Rockies in the winter and returned to the high country each summer to harvest animals. After Native Americans acquired horses in the early 1700s, tribes became nomadic and moved onto the plains to follow migrating herds of bison.

A Native American trail on Coal Creek southeast of Lafayette was an important route for settlers. Waneka said that the Harmons, pre-Lafayette homesteaders who lived near town founder Mary Miller's farm, pushed their cart along the streamside trail to procure supplies in Louisville, as did the Barrowmans, who lived along Coal Creek near the present-day Erie Airpark. As early as 1868, Denver industrialists eyed the Coal Creek Valley streamside route for rail service connecting Boulder with Denver.

Among Colorado's most significant trails was the Cherokee Trail, a portion of which followed what is now U.S. Highway 287 north from Broomfield to Lafayette. North of Lafayette, the Cherokee Trail veered northwest toward White Rock and Niwot, then skirted the west side of Longmont, Loveland and Fort Collins.

Historian Elliot West, author of *The Contested Plains*, described the Cherokee Trail as "an ancient road" that went north–south along the base of the Rocky Mountains. "For hundreds of generations before Coronado, nomadic hunters and traders had passed up and down the trough below the Front Range," wrote West.

The nine-hundred-mile Cherokee Trail started at Tahlequah, Oklahoma, and headed north to central Kansas, where it turned west and followed the Arkansas River to Pueblo. From Pueblo, the trail hugged the Front Range through Colorado Springs, Denver, Lafayette, Longmont, LaPorte and then Virginia Dale. In Wyoming, the Cherokee Trail headed west from (New) Laramie over the Medicine Bow Range and terminated at Fort Bridger outside of Ogden, Utah.

The Cherokee Trail was named for Native American migrants who trekked from Indian Territory in Oklahoma to California seeking gold. The trailblazer was Captain Lewis Evans (1799–1879), who in 1849 led the first forty-wagon train composed of 124 people, including 14 Cherokees, 5 African slaves and 3 women. That group followed the east side of the South Platte River along the Front Range and headed west at the mouth of the Cache la Poudre River.

Four groups of migrants, including one composed of 105 men and 12 women and diarized by Cherokee John Lowery Brown (1770–1852), left Tahlequah in 1850 and crossed the South Platte at Denver, then headed north through Lafayette and on to LaPorte. Brown's group is credited with the first documented discovery of gold along "Ralston's Creek" near Denver. Thousands of migrants and gold seekers from Arkansas, Texas, Missouri and the Cherokee Nation used the trail in following years.

Segments of the Cherokee Trail overlapped other established trails, including the Santa Fe Trail and the Santa Fe/Taos to Fort Laramie Trail, also known as Trappers Trail. The wagon road was also known as the Great Ware (War) Road, the California Road and the Arkansas Emigrant Trail.

Government survey crews from the General Land Office documented the Cherokee Trail through eastern Boulder County in the summer of 1859 and labeled the trail "Salt Lake to Santa Fe."

The survey crews returned in 1864 and termed the trail the "Laramie Road," which refers to the fur-trading route—also called Trappers Trail—from Santa Fe/Taos to Fort Laramie, a frontier outpost established in eastern Wyoming in the 1830s.

An alternate segment of Trappers Trail followed the South Platte River in eastern Colorado, but historical records (at right in accompanying image) describe prospectors camping on the Santa Fe/Taos to Fort Laramie Trail next to the Cache la Poudre River in LaPorte.

FROM 1862 TO 1870, settlers dotting the prairie north of Denver and along Colorado's Front Range were treated to a technological marvel known as the stagecoach. At the time, witnessing a bright red Abbot Downing Concord Coach gliding over the open grasslands with a driver at the reins, a messenger by his side guarding the strongbox and up to twelve passengers being pulled by six powerful horses was akin to witnessing the Orient Express chug its way out of the Constantinople train station.

Concord stagecoaches were built in Concord, New Hampshire, and featured large, oak wagon wheels and a rounded passenger compartment suspended on multilayered oxhide straps. Side windows were open, with cloth or canvas curtains that could be rolled down in bad weather. The interior featured three upholstered bench seats. Passengers were allowed twenty-one pounds of luggage.

The U.S. government sponsored the first wagon transport of mail, known as the "Hockaday Line," through the Great American Desert in 1848, a 1,200-mile journey over what was called the Overland Route from Independence, Missouri, to Salt Lake City. From Independence, the route

Men pose on a horse-drawn stagecoach that belonged to Wells, Fargo and Company at Kimball's stage stop outside of Salt Lake City in 1867. The stagecoach would have passed through what is now Lafayette on the run between Denver and Salt Lake City. *Denver Public Library, Western History Collection, X-21823.*

Abner C. and Clara Goodhue (*right*) sit with Pat Kilker, Bone Kilker and Annie Eberle on the front porch of the Miller Tavern at Stearns Dairy (Rock Creek Farm) along Rock Creek, south of Lafayette. Abner bought the tavern, a stop on the Denver-to-Cheyenne stage route, from Lafayette and Mary Miller in 1871. *Lafayette Public Library*.

went northwest to Atchison, Kansas, then to Fort Kearney, Nebraska, then to Fort Laramie in southeast Wyoming, then along the North Platte River to Bridger's Pass and Fort Bridger in southwest Wyoming, then to Salt Lake. Ten years later, stagecoaches started hauling both mail and passengers along the route.

In 1861, entrepreneur Ben Holladay won the U.S. Postal Service's mail-hauling contract for Missouri to Salt Lake City and launched the Overland Stage Line, which later became the Overland Mail and Express Company. In 1862, an alliance of Arapaho and Sioux forced Holladay's stagecoaches southward from the Overland Route to what would be termed the Southern Overland Route (and, later, the Overland Trail Denver Loop).

Starting in 1864, stagecoaches turned south at Fort Kearney, then followed the South Platte River to Denver. From there, the stagecoaches picked up the Cherokee Trail/Laramie Road, the main north–south dirt roadway. Two years before the major route change, a November 1862 *Rocky Mountain News* story detailed a stagecoach journey from Denver to Salt Lake City. "We cannot close this article without a passing tribute to the admirable condition and excellent management of Ben Holladay's Overland Stage Line. When it is remembered that during the last summer an entire new and before untraveled road was opened from this city [Denver] through Bridger's Pass," stated the article.

From 1864 to 1868, the Cherokee Trail/Laramie Road was a principal travel corridor to the west and a key part of the Overland Mail and Express Company's one-thousand-mile route, which originated in Atchison. The Front Range portion of the Southern Route went north from Denver to LaPorte and Virginia Dale, where the trail rejoined the Central Overland Route in Laramie.

The Overland Mail and Express Company's six-hundred-mile Denver to Salt Lake City Division comprised forty-six stage stations spaced every ten to fifteen miles. Station operators grew and cut hay and stored grain for Ben Holladay's 1,700 stagecoach horses and mules. The stage would pull into the station, and the operator would swap the worn-out horses for fresh ones. Horses and mules were swapped every ten to fifteen miles depending on terrain and weather conditions. Stagecoaches averaged sixty to one hundred miles a day. Stage drivers preferred mules because of their stamina and strength when navigating sandy creek bottoms.

Home stations and division stations served food, while the smaller swing stations were all about the livestock. This meant that the swing station operator was on call for a stage arriving at late hours. Stagecoaches left Denver and Salt Lake City every ten hours and wheeled along the trail twenty-four hours a day, regardless of weather. Overland Express Company stagecoaches did not make overnight stops, so passengers slept the best they could over the rough terrain. The stagecoach driver often seat-belted himself to the driver's seat, the "box," which enabled him to sleep as long as forty-five minutes while driving.

Many Overland Express Company home and division stations had overnight accommodations, but a passenger disembarking the stagecoach for a clean bed had no guarantee of getting on any following stagecoach. Stagecoaches heading west from Denver almost always had waiting lists.

The stagecoach crossing at Boulder Creek north of Lafayette was at today's North 109th Street near Brownsville, about one-half mile east of U.S. Highway 287. Starting in 1864, three Overland Stage Line stations in Boulder and Broomfield Counties operated under the purview of Ben Holladay's Overland Mail and Express Company: Little Thompson stage station, about two miles north of today's Longmont; Boon's Ranch (Boulder

Station) stage station at Boulder Creek; and Church's Ranch stage station (then called Child's stage station), located near today's Old Wadsworth and 105th Street in Westminster. The Burlington House in what is now Longmont became an Overland Stage Line home station a few years later.

In the late 1860s, roadside taverns along the Denver to Salt Lake City stagecoach route served as meal stops. Menus included liquor, coffee, wild game, fried salt pork, biscuits and occasionally fresh vegetables and fruit.

From 1866 to 1871, Lafayette and Mary Miller operated the Miller Tavern Ranch, a saloon and stage stop at the former Stearns Dairy north of Dillon Road on U.S. 287, today known as the Rock Creek Farm.

The Mason & Ganow stagecoach company launched on October 17, 1868, to compete with Wells Fargo. It promoted daily overnight service from Denver to Cheyenne, about one hundred miles. Heading north, the stagecoach left Denver at 8:00 a.m. and arrived in Cheyenne at 7:00 a.m. the next morning. Traveling south, the stagecoach left Cheyenne at 6:00 p.m.

Lafayette pioneers Adolf and Anna Waneka ran the two-story stage stop on Coal Creek located where today's U.S. 287 crosses Coal Creek in Lafayette, but it, too, was a meal stop and not a swing station.

THE *ROCKY MOUNTAIN NEWS* for November 19, 1867, listed six stage companies operating from Denver: Wells, Fargo & Company, with stages leaving daily for points east via the Platte and points west via Salt Lake City; Denver, Valmont and Boulder stage company, leaving Thursdays and Saturdays; United States Express Company, leaving daily for points east via Smoky Hill route; Hariman & Harmon's stage, leaving for South Park each Thursday; Denver, Idaho and Georgetown Express, leaving Denver Tuesdays, Thursdays and Saturdays; and the Denver and Santa Fe Stage Line, leaving Denver for points south every Monday, Wednesday and Friday.

Ben Holladay's Overland Mail and Express Company was sold to Wells, Fargo & Company in 1866 for $1.8 million in cash and stocks. After the Transcontinental Railroad was completed to Cheyenne in 1867, stagecoach travel declined, and the majority of stagecoaches heading from Denver to Cheyenne carried passengers looking to catch an eastbound train.

By early 1869, Wells Fargo had sold all of its stagecoach operations, including the Denver to Cheyenne run, which was acquired by John Hughes. Robert Spotswood and William McClelland bought the stage line from Hughes and continued running the Denver to Cheyenne stage until November 27, 1869.

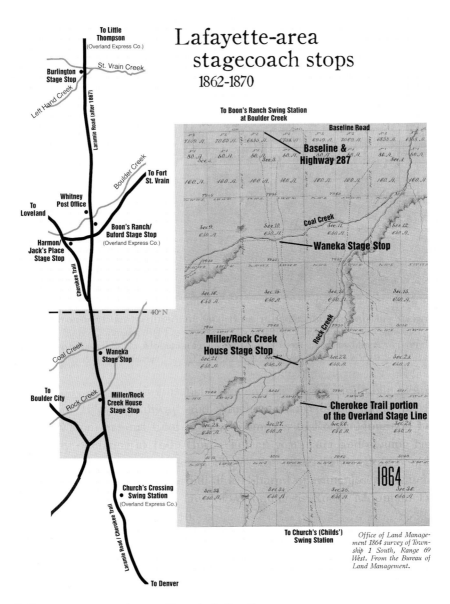

Lafayette area stagecoach stops. *Illustration by the author.*

Denver City in the early 1860s was a bustling place. Thousands of gold prospectors were arriving daily from the East, eager to load up on provisions for their continued treks to the gold and silver areas west of the growing Colorado Territory city.

Hyatt Hussey arrived in Denver City around 1864, bringing with him a background in banking and finance. For businessmen venturing west from Missouri, Kansas, Nebraska and Iowa, there was just as much money to be made providing products and services to prospectors as there was in being a prospector—but without losing life or limb in a mine shaft.

In 1866, Hussey helped form the first fire department in Denver, the Denver Hook & Ladder No. 1. A few years after the General Land Office's township and section survey was completed in 1865, Hussey set out from Denver on horseback to explore the areas near the Boulder County hard rock mining camps. Hussey veered off the Cherokee Trail and picked up the single-track Indian trail along Coal Creek, starting at the confluence of Coal Creek and Boulder Creek, and then worked his way west to the mouth of Coal Creek Canyon above Rocky Flats.

Like the 1864 and 1865 government surveyors, Hussey would have noticed a wide swath of fields under cultivation on both sides of the creek. A handful of farmhouses and cattle dotted the horizon, with primitive stacked log fences enclosing pastures. Continuing along the streamside trail, Hussey would have passed by the Waneka Stage Stop and may have stopped for a meal and enjoyed the hospitality of Adolf and Anna Waneka.

The Coal Creek Valley streamside route would have been relatively level, free of trees and other obstructions and passed conveniently close to the area's first coal mines in Marshall, where coal was mined starting in 1859. For Hussey, it was the perfect route for a new railroad line.

On May 8, 1868, Hussey and his business associates Court C. Clements and Chambers C. Davis filed articles of incorporation in the Boulder County Clerk's office for the Coal Creek Valley Railroad Company, whose purpose was "constructing, operating and maintaining a rail road line… starting in Township 1 South of Range 70 West at or near the base of the Rocky Mountains thence by the most feasible route down the valley of Coal Creek back to a point on said creek at or near the Range sixty eight and sixty nine thence by the nearest feasible route to the valley of Dry Creek to the South Platte river thence across said river to a point of connection south of the river to the Denver Pacific Railway and Telegraph Company."

The three Denver entrepreneurs probably had a simple premise: If they could get coal from the mines sprouting next to Coal Creek to eager customers in Denver City, and even to points beyond, the rewards would be substantial. For the moment, Lafayette would be left out of the railroad boom.

The Coal Creek Valley Railroad Company had initial capital valued at $500,000 and was the first Boulder County railway company and among the first dozen railroad associations formed in the Colorado Territory, the first being the Denver and Arkansas Air Line Road, which incorporated in April 1865.

An east–west railroad route along Boulder Creek starting in Brighton and terminating in Erie was built by Denver, Utah & Pacific Railroad in 1871. That line, known as the Boulder Valley, transported Canfield coal used primarily for Denver Pacific locomotives. In 1873, the rail line continued west through Canfield and Valmont and terminated in Boulder. A north–south route from Denver to Boulder via Golden and Louisville was also completed in 1873 by the Colorado Central Railroad, which became the Union Pacific, Denver and Gulf Railway in 1890. A subsidiary of the Union Pacific, the Denver Marshall & Boulder Railway, built a direct route from Denver to Louisville and Boulder in 1885 and bypassed Golden. The Marshall & Boulder link went through Church Ranch and Broomfield. After the Union Pacific went bankrupt in 1893, the railway became the Colorado & Southern. The Colorado Central route connected to Cheyenne in 1877 and (as C&S) eventually connected Denver to Laramie via the Front Range. Louis Nawatny, who platted and named Louisville after himself in 1878, was a surveyor for Colorado Central and helped sink the Welch coal mine east of Louisville.

Nothing ever became of the Coal Creek Valley Railroad Company. In 1871, Hussey helped build the Denver Opera House and acted as treasurer for the Denver Opera House Association. He'd held a steady job at the City National Bank in Denver City but retired from the bank and became a Denver coal dealer, selling Marshall coal at Fifteenth and Lawrence in Denver starting in 1878.

The first passenger railroad in the United States, the Baltimore & Ohio, commenced construction in 1828. By the 1870s, over eighty thousand miles of railroad track had been laid. Facilitated by federal land grants, the ambitious Transcontinental Railroad was built westward from Omaha by the Union Pacific Railroad and built eastward by the Central Pacific Railroad based in Sacramento.

In exchange for taking the risk to build a railroad line, the U.S. government allowed railroad companies to claim five alternate sections per mile, within five miles of each side of a railroad line. These were usually

Chicago, Burlington & Quincy locomotive 5090 photographed in Lafayette on November 12, 1951, by George A. Trout. *Denver Public Library, Western History Collection, Z-10931.*

odd-numbered sections. Sections already homesteaded or preempted were exempt from railroad claims.

The Transcontinental routes linked up in Promontory, Utah, in 1869. A year later, the Denver Pacific Railroad connected Denver to Cheyenne and the Union Pacific.

The Boulder Valley Railway, affiliated with the Denver Pacific, opened in Erie in 1871 and extended to Boulder in 1874. Prior to the opening of the Erie market, coal hauled to Denver in wagons sold at a retail price of ten to fifteen dollars per ton. After the opening of the railroad, coal dropped to four dollars per ton.

The Denver Marshall & Boulder Railway (a Union Pacific, Denver and Gulf Railway subsidiary that eventually became a part of the Colorado & Southern) was the first railroad brought to Lafayette in 1889 by John H. Simpson, who sank the Simpson Mine with his father and brothers and the Spencer Mine with partner Charles Spencer. The three-mile spur connected Lafayette to Louisville and points beyond.

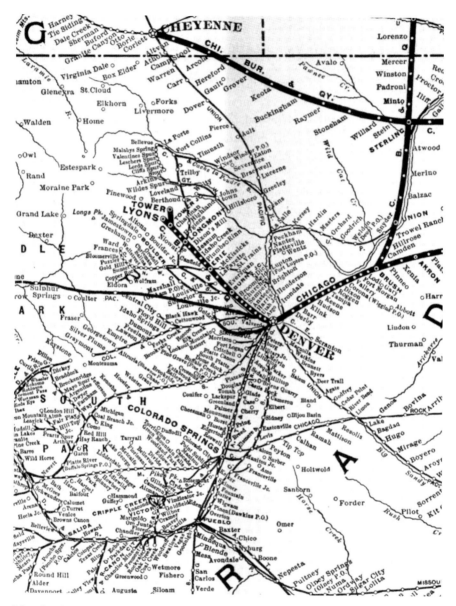

Map showing the Denver-to-Lyons passenger train excursion route through Lafayette. *Burlington Route Colorado and Utah Handbook for Pleasure Seekers, 1906.* Chicago, Burlington & Quincy Railroad Company, 1906. Chicago: Poole Brothers Publishing.

The Union Pacific/C&S spur from Louisville to Lafayette originated at roughly Pine Street in Louisville, then headed northeast to Lafayette, crossing Public Road at Emma Street, then about another half mile, where it terminated at the Spencer and Simpson Mines on the east edge of Lafayette. The Strathmore Mine and Cannon Mine were connected to the spur, and today's Emma Street heading east from Public Road is slightly bow-shaped because it follows the track bed that was built for the Cannon Mine railroad spur.

The C&S depot was located in the middle of what is now Finch Avenue between Cleveland and Cannon Streets. A few years later, John H. Simpson helped the Burlington & Missouri River Railroad build along the eastern edge of town. The Lafayette depot for the B&M, which eventually became Burlington Northern, was located at what is today the intersection of Simpson Street and Burlington Avenue.

In 1898, five trains per day, carrying mostly coal, ran between Lafayette and Denver. Sunday passenger trains ran between Lyons and Denver. A shopping excursion from Lafayette to Denver was as easy a grabbing the 8:17 a.m. train and returning on the 6:01 p.m. train. The fare was three and a half cents per mile.

Trains hauled lots of freight, too. Red sandstone hauled from Lyons and factory bricks from Boulder were used to build Lafayette's first houses and businesses. But the railroad's main moneymaker was hauling coal from area mines. In 1895, coal hauled from Louisville to Denver produced $300,000 in revenues for the railroad. By 1906, the peak year of production for the Simpson Mine, the two railroads serving Lafayette were transporting to Denver over two thousand tons of Lafayette-area coal, about one hundred coal cars, every day.

THE C&S RAILROAD RAN a passenger train five times daily between Lafayette and Louisville. C&S also owned the Denver & Interurban Railroad Company, a heavy passenger trolley known as the "Kite Route" that was powered by overhead electrical lines originating at Lafayette's Interurban Power Plant at Waneka Lake. Starting in 1908, the D&I made eighteen daily round trips between Denver and Boulder, through Louisville, on C&S tracks. In later years, the D&I ran every two hours from 5:30 a.m. to 11:00 p.m. The transit company was closed in 1932.

For two brief years, the (official) Lincoln Highway came through Lafayette. Conceived in 1913 as a direct motor route between the West Coast and the East Coast, the Lincoln Highway became the first cross-country roadway. At conception, the road traversed California, Nevada, Utah, Wyoming, Nebraska, Iowa, Illinois, Indiana, Ohio, West Virginia, Pennsylvania, New Jersey and New York. A designation of an alternate route, or loop, from Cheyenne to Denver, then back up to Julesburg was also included in the initial route.

Lafayette was on the route of the Cheyenne to Denver leg, but in 1915, the Lincoln Highway Association formally withdrew sanction for the "Denver Loop." Colorado's governor Elias Ammons protested the delisting, but the association prevailed.

The short-lived northbound route of the Lincoln Highway through Lafayette followed Public Road to Baseline Road; left on Baseline to 111th; right on 111th to Isabelle Road; left on Isabelle to 109th; north on 109th and then left at Lookout Road (at the time called "Six Mile Corner"); then right onto what is now U.S. Highway 287.

Unfortunately, Lafayette boosters never got the memo detailing the unlisting of the Denver Loop. Undaunted, the community designated Public Road the "Lincoln Highway," and the moniker stuck for several decades.

The summer of 1926 featured a fierce battle between Longmont and Boulder over the tourist trade.

That summer, the route of the future Highway 287 north from Lafayette was being firmed up by Colorado transportation officials, who wanted to change the previous Lincoln Highway route out of Lafayette. At the time, the Lincoln Highway followed today's 111th Avenue next to the Lafayette Cemetery. In 1913, the 111th route was designated a part of the transcontinental Lincoln Highway, but all segments of the Colorado loop were delisted in 1915 by the Lincoln Highway Association. For several decades after that, locals still referred to the road as the Lincoln Highway.

One mile north of 111th and Baseline, the intersection of Arapahoe and 111th was known as Ten Mile Corner. The reference was distance to Longmont, not Boulder. Four miles north of that intersection, accessed via the notorious "Dead Man's Curve," was Six Mile Corner at Lookout Road and 109th. A mile north of that (and five miles north of Ten Mile Corner and five miles south of Longmont) was Five Mile Corner, now the intersection of Highway 52 and Highway 287.

The only highway access from Denver to Boulder at the time went through Ten Mile Corner, the intersection of Arapahoe Road and 111th. Because all traffic headed to Rocky Mountain National Park and northern Colorado also went through the intersection, Ten Mile Corner was a busy one—so much so that the Boulder Chamber of Commerce erected a small tourist hut to direct drivers westward on Arapahoe Road, which they claimed was the best route to Estes Park.

In response to the tourist hut, the Longmont Chamber of Commerce announced in the July 10, 1926 *Longmont Daily Times* that it intended to build a ten-foot-tall-by-forty-foot-wide road map sign at Ten Mile Corner. The large map would direct drivers north to Estes Park via Longmont, not Boulder.

A week later, on July 17, the *Daily Times* reported that the Boulder tourist hut at Ten Mile Corner had burned to the ground. Troublemakers from Longmont were initially suspected, but Boulder citizens came forward and said they themselves had burned it down "out of a spirit of fairness to other northern Colorado cities."

The *Daily Times* stated in the July 17 report that it hoped the removal of the shed "will be termed a closed incident and that in the future all will confine themselves to only fair and legitimate methods when making a bid for the tourist and his business."

The large Longmont road map billboard was never built.

In 1927, the route of the old Lincoln Highway was changed to go west on Baseline Road out of Lafayette to the current location of Highway 287 (then called Highway 87). It then went straight north into Longmont.

With the goal of diverting the tourist trade to Boulder, sometime in 1927, the name "Nine Mile Corner" was assigned to the completed intersection of Highway 287 and Arapahoe Road. Although Nine Mile Corner was only a half mile west of Ten Mile Corner, Nine Mile Corner referenced the distance to downtown Boulder.

And in late 1927 and early 1928, Boulder got the final say in directing the tourist trade to Estes Park. The Boulder Lions Club installed two large stone memorial pillars (in remembrance of veterans of World War I) at Nine Mile Corner. A *Y* intersection built at the same time made it difficult to go any direction other than east on Arapahoe, accommodated by the placement of a large cannon in the middle of the *Y*—essentially the middle of Highway 287. The pillars still flank Arapahoe Road today.

8

A UNION TOWN

At the peak of local coal production in the 1910s, coal miners had one thing in common: they all carried union cards. Lafayette was the epicenter of organized labor's struggle for fair wages and a safe workplace.

During the six decades of Lafayette's commercialized coal mining (1888 to 1946), coal miners had one consistent complaint: being shorted of hard-earned wages when their coal was weighed. Unlike a hard-rock miner who was able to observe the assayer weigh his precious few grains of gold or silver, the coal miner—who was paid by the ton—had to trust that the coal being weighed several hundred feet above his workplace was done so accurately.

Until 1907, a miner's pit car of coal was weighed after it had been dumped into railroad cars, first passing through a series of sorting screens. Early coal miners were paid only for the higher-quality lump coal, which was the coal used for home heating. In the tipple, the miner's roughly two-thousand-pound load of coal filtered through a series of sloped screens, and the coal fell into three open railroad cars sitting on large scales. Because of the screening method, up to 25 percent of the miner's coal was classified as undesirable "nut coal," and the miner wasn't paid for it.

While it was easy for the company's weighboss to short the miner's haul simply by unbalancing the scales, some miners were credited for more coal than they mined. This occurred when workers employed to redistribute the

United Mine Workers of America union hall at Gough Avenue and East Simpson Street, 1909. *Author's collection.*

coal jumped on and off the railroad car holding the lump coal. When they stayed on the railroad car—thus on the scale—as it was being weighed, it added 150 to 400 pounds to the miner's tally.

Enacted in 1907, the Colorado Statute Law in Relation to Coal Mines, Section 3204k, mandated the "run of mine" system: that the coal be weighed "before it is screened or before it is passed over or dumped on any screen" and that the miner be paid for all of the coal contained in his pit car, not just the lump coal.

In 1911, coal operators lobbied the state legislature to change the coal-weighing system back to the "old fashioned" railroad car method, but then Governor John F. Shafroth vetoed the bill.

THE 1916 U.S. COMMISSION on Industrial Relations noted that Colorado coal miners' strikes occurred once every nine to ten years.

Strikes during the 1890s centered on unfairness in the weighing of coal and on the introduction of scrip as a payment method. Introduced in 1892–93 by coal operators who were struggling to pay miners—some three months in arrears—company scrip was a credit voucher of sorts that could be spent only at company-owned stores.

In 1912, Rocky Mountain Fuel Company executives maintained that they issued "coupons" rather than scrip and that the coupons were merely a substitute for cash. Miners maintained that they risked losing their jobs if they didn't accept and redeem the company voucher at the company store. The scrip concept of paying miners continued for several decades, to as late as 1927, when Rocky Mountain Fuel Company's Josephine Roche halted the practice.

In addition to questions of fairness in weighing, most pre-1900s disputes centered on fairness of wages. After 1900, safety issues, particularly the quality of the air distributed in the mine by large fans on the surface, became contentious.

Until about 1910, miners had no legal recourse when it came to death or dismemberment in the workplace. Mine owners were not held responsible for accidents; the miner himself was to blame. The mine owners' excuse went something like this: "This is inherently dangerous work and the miner knew that the ceiling over the coal face was unsafe but he chose to continue to work. We can't be held responsible for that."

Mine safety and workers' compensation laws slowly shifted the safety burden to the owners. When miners felt that safety laws weren't being enforced, they went out on strike.

THE FIRST U.S. FEDERAL Census in the Lafayette area to show coal mining as a vocation was the Louisville Precinct census of June 1880. Almost three-quarters of the vocations listed in Louisville were for coal mining. After Louisville was inventoried by the census taker, he walked east along Coal Creek, first interviewing Adolf Waneka, then age fifty-four, and his son Henry "Boye" Waneka. About a mile from the Wanekas, Manning and Julia Harmon were next, followed by John B. Foote, Mary Miller's father, who had established the Foote-Miller Farm along with James B. Foote at roughly today's South Boulder Road and South Public Road. Lafayette Miller died in Boulder in 1878, so Mary, age thirty-eight, moved back to her east Boulder County farm. She and her six children were listed in 1880 as residing in the John B. Foote household.

Benjamin Prutchcroux, a French immigrant, is listed as a farmer residing along Coal Creek east of the Foote-Miller Farm. Adjacent to Prutchcroux, probably directly east of today's Lafayette, residents Alex McPherson, Alex Bailey, Jesse Bower, George Cowdrie, George Howe and John Howe are listed as "coal miners" and can be considered Lafayette's first coal miners.

One of the most hazardous vocations on record, early coal mining was nothing more than men with picks undercutting hundreds of feet of rock to extract a narrow seam of coal. The room-and-pillar system for removing coal was highly productive but very dangerous. Some coal was left in place to support the rock layers, and thousands of wood timbers were used to brace the rock above the voids so that the coal could be loaded. Dislodging the coal involved a miner bringing his own keg of black powder into the mine, which, when packed into drilled holes, could detonate prematurely or not at all. Miners worked separate rooms sometimes miles from the main shaft, which meant little supervision. Add to this the pay-per-ton wages, wherein a miner often overlooked his own safety so that as much coal as possible could be loaded.

What could possibly go wrong?

From 1890 to 1894, American bituminous coal miners were killed at almost twice the rate of their British counterparts: 2.52 fatalities per 1,000 workers per year in the U.S. versus 1.61 per 1,000 workers in the UK. Only the fatality rate for nineteenth-century railroad workers, 6.45 fatalities per 1,000 workers in 1895, surpassed the rate of mining fatalities. High railroad employee fatality rates were attributed to workers being required to stand between cars to couple and uncouple them.

During Lafayette's coal-mining era (1887 to 1956), the town's most dangerous mine by far was the Cannon/Otis, which averaged one death per 43,000 tons of coal mined during its ten-year history. The Spencer-Simpson Mine averaged one death per 330,000 tons of coal mined, and the Columbine Mine averaged one death per 318,000 tons of coal.

In dozens of Lafayette oral history interviews conducted in the 1970s and 1980s by the late Effie Amicarella and others, an oft-asked question of long-passed coal miners was whether they had enjoyed their work. Some didn't mind the work, because the weather at the coal face was predictable. The temperature two hundred feet below the surface was a consistent fifty degrees, which was warm on cold winter days and cool on hotter spring days.

Other miners hated the job. Because coal dust was ever present, it was dark except for the light generated by a helmet lamp—first an oil lamp, then, in later years, an electric carbide lamp. And the work was backbreaking. Until 1900, pick mining relied on a miner hand-digging and undercutting the coal face, laying in dampness on his side. When undercutting machines run by compressed air started being used after 1900, the undercutting got easier, but the loading of the coal into a coal car still relied on a shovel and the muscles and strong back of a miner.

What miners feared most was being overcome by or igniting mine gas, also known as "firedamp." Northern Field coal mines were recognized as being less prone to "gassiness," and accident reports from area mines reflected that most injuries and deaths were due to rockfall and coal car mishaps versus suffocation or mine gas explosions. Gas did accumulate in Boulder and Weld County coal mines, just not in the same heavy concentration as at Las Animas County and other southern Colorado coal mines.

Mining laws adopted in the late 1880s required that Colorado coal mines provide adequate air circulation to prevent buildup of CH_4, commonly known as methane, a highly explosive yet odorless and colorless gas produced from the biodegradation of organic material.

After excavating fifteen thousand square yards of coal and rock, the mine was expected to have at least one airshaft in addition to the main shaft, and dual haulageways emanating outward from the main shaft needed crosscuts connecting the haulageways every fifty feet. A large ventilation fan at the surface forced air into the mine and was combined with doors and brattice cloth in the mine that helped direct fresh air to coal faces being worked.

Other state safety measures, including when, where and by whom a coal shot could be fired, were slow in coming. Even after Colorado mining laws were enacted, coal operators were continually accused by miners of not following them. Since fines for not following state law were small, operators often paid them and then continued the bad or unsafe practice. Additionally, state mine inspectors had to have permission to enter mine property.

What did change operators' attitude toward workplace safety was the shift in workplace monetary settlements after a miner was killed or injured. Until 1900, only half of workers injured in the workplace recovered damages. Settlements usually amounted to about half a year's worth of pay. When the state's workers' compensation program was enacted, the cost of an accident became much more expensive. Not only did operators have to pay into a workers' compensation pool, which added overhead, but they were also required to compensate employees for injuries sustained on the job. A workplace fatality that at one time cost no more than $200 jumped to $2,000.

Hitting the coal producers in the pocketbook is largely the reason that coal mine safety improved.

The extended and sometimes violent strike of 1910–14, called the "Long Strike," taxed Lafayette. Miners belonging to the United Mine Workers of America were determined to get fair wages and safety improvements in a dangerous workplace, while operators wanted the mined coal to continue flowing. Both sides were heavily armed and ready to draw at the first provocation.

Until about 1910, labor disputes did not center on dangerous working conditions.

Common law at the turn of the twentieth century placed prevention of workplace accidents squarely on the worker and not the employer. The assumption of risk was the miner's—if a coal miner was injured or killed, it was his fault. Colorado mining law enacted in 1883 stated that "where a miner knowingly and voluntarily exposes himself to the falling of a defective roof, which he has inspected and found to be so defective that a miner of common prudence should deem it unsafe, his negligence must be held willful and sufficient to preclude his recovery for an injury brought upon himself for such exposure." After 1910, case law decided in state courts shifted the burden of an unsafe working environment to the employer, which meant that operators had to make a reasonable effort to keep miners out of dangerous areas of the mine. The Colorado General Assembly would not establish workers' compensation until 1915.

In the Northern Field, the "Long Strike" started on April 1, 1910. UMWA miners wanted an increase of $0.03 per ton for machine mining,

Strikebreakers at the Vulcan coal mine south of Lafayette, about 1911. *Denver Public Library, Western History Collection, X-60581.*

$0.04 for pick mining, a 5.55 percent increase for day wages and dead work, an eight-hour workday, selection of checkweighmen, union recognition and enforcement of state labor and mine safety laws. In 1912, the Colorado Bureau of Labor Statistics estimated the average wage for a Colorado coal miner was $1.68 per day.

As was the case in previous strikes, miners accused operators of shorting their pay. Miners were paid by the ton, and the striking miners alleged that—even with checkweighmen selected and paid by the miners—company weighbosses were still shorting the weight, depriving miners what they earned. An 1897 law passed by the Colorado General Assembly said that miners could select the checkweighman and pay him out of their own wages. Operators countered that the turnover in some mines was so great that it was almost impossible to collect adequate wages to cover the checkweighman's wages. Additionally, the misdemeanor penalty for failure to comply with mining laws amounted to only a few dollars, so the law was largely ignored by operators.

At a convention in Trinidad in September 1913, UMWA delegates from across the state endorsed a statewide strike, which became the greatest labor upheaval in Colorado history. Coal miners statewide accused operators of favoring profits over the safety of workers, and their demands included coal operators' recognition of the union, an increase in wages of 10 percent, an eight-hour workday for all classes of labor in or around the coal mines, payment for dead work, the right to have union-paid weighbosses, the right of the miners to trade wherever they pleased (instead of at company stores), the right to choose their own boarding place and their own doctor, the enforcement of the Colorado mining laws and "total abolition of the notorious and criminal guard system."

During the strike, Rocky Mountain Fuel Company, owners of the Simpson and Vulcan Mines in Lafayette, the Acme Mine in Louisville and the Industrial Mine in Superior, recruited and paid the railroad fare for nonunion coal miners from West Virginia, Tennessee, Kentucky and Joplin, Missouri. Strikebreakers were labeled either "scabs" or "blacklegs." Those on strike, members of the United Miner Workers of America, were called "rednecks," because they wore red handkerchiefs around their necks. After asking Boulder County sheriff M.P. Capp to deputize up to seventy-five company men to help guard the mines, which he refused, Northern Coal and Coke Company hired West Virginia–based Baldwin-Felts Detective Agency guards to protect the company's assets. The Baldwin-Felts guards, known in southern coal states for protecting coal trains and payroll shipments, were hired to prevent trespassing on company property.

After the 1898 coal miners' strike, the operators had learned a hard lesson: If they hired nonunion strikebreakers, they needed to keep them separated from the striking union men. Before the 1910 strike, the Simpson Mine had only one or two structures for housing miners on-site. Managers and engineers were housed in company homes on the north side of the mine, but the vast majority of miners lived in residential areas of Lafayette. A few weeks after union miners walked off the job in 1910, Northern Coal and Coke Company started building six-foot barbed-wire fences on the perimeters of their mine properties. At the Simpson Mine, the company drew plans for the town of Simpson, Colorado—separate from Lafayette— that included a barbed-wire fence surrounding newly built housing for the strikebreakers' families, a hotel for the single men and a casino for on-site entertainment. Striking miners labeled the mines "stockades" or "bullpens" because of the fortress-like fences.

Over a fifty-week period from 1910 to 1911, Northern Coal and Coke Company jammed thirty-six houses, four bunkhouses and one boardinghouse onto a level field south of the Simpson tipple.

During the frequent coal strikes dating back to shortly after area mines opened in the 1880s, miners didn't consider the engineers and mechanics who continued to work during the strike as scabs, nor were they mistreated or confronted in the community. The striking miners knew that the mine equipment needed to be maintained and needed to be in good working order once the strike was settled.

In the early years of the 1910–14 strike, Bulgarians, Mexicans and Greeks were brought in to replace the striking Welsh, American, Italian and Slavic miners. Lafayette coal miner Henry "Welchie" Mathias (1894–1978) recalled that the strikebreakers "arrived on trains and the windows would be whitewashed or chalked up 'till they got right to the mine, drive the goddamn train coach right to the mines and unload them." Coal miner Cliff Alderson (1907–1995) recalled that scabs being transported by train hid behind stacked timbers lining boxcars so they wouldn't be hit by random bullets fired from trackside by union sympathizers.

The first violent clash between union sympathizers and strikers occurred on August 15, 1910, at the Burlington railroad depot in east Lafayette when mine guard Bomen Fowler was shot by Town Marshal John P. "Jack" Cassidy.

Fowler was accompanying the Standard Mine's secretary, E.E. Bean, and both were escorting a newly hired guard for the mine. Standard Mine was about a mile east of the Simpson Mine and was also surrounded by a six-foot barbed-wire fence.

When union miners confronted the Standard Mine trio as they were exiting a Burlington train, Fowler struck one of the union miners. Cassidy observed the confrontation and ordered Fowler to throw up his hands. Fowler disobeyed, and Cassidy's gun accidentally discharged as he was drawing it on Fowler to arrest him. Fowler's injuries were minor, but he was taken by buggy to the town doctor.

The next day, union miners and Boulder County sheriff M.P. Capp traveled to Denver to visit Colorado governor John F. Shafroth. Capp told the governor that no outside help was needed. The union miners assured Shafroth that miners would strike on peaceful terms. According to the August 19, 1910 *Lafayette Leader*, Governor Shafroth expressed confidence that the provisions of the strike agreement reached between the union miners and the mine companies would be followed. The agreement was that the miners were to stay away from the companies' properties and that company guards would refrain from leaving the mine premises. Mine owners, however, told Shafroth that their "property and men were menaced continually" by the striking union members.

At the request of Shafroth, Colorado secretary of state James B. Pearce visited Lafayette in late August 1910 and praised Sheriff Capp for his handling of the strike. "With more than 2,000 men on strike for more than four months, the county has been quiet as if no strike existed," Pearce told the *Denver News*. "I found cases…where children would shout 'scab' to try to annoy miners who were at work. In not one instance did I find a man who thought there was any necessity for the governor to intervene in the matter."

In September 1910, coal operators, including RM Fuel's E.E. Shumway, asked Denver District Court judge Greeley W. Whitford to issue an injunction to restrain striking miners from gathering in groups, posting notices or interfering with nonunion operation of the mines. Whitford agreed to the injunction and appointed Baldwin-Felts detectives as enforcers.

The *Lafayette Leader* wrote that on October 5, 1910, men from the Standard Mine, under the leadership of the Baldwin-Felts Detective Agency, came up from the mine to "take the town." Thirty strikebreakers marched into town at sundown accompanied by Baldwin detectives in an automobile.

"Hardly had the marchers set foot inside city limits when the news spread like wildfire," reported the *Lafayette Leader*. "From every house and cottage streamed men armed to the teeth ready to defend their town, their homes and their families to the best of their abilities."

Sheriff M.P. Capp confronted the marchers as they climbed Simpson Street toward the saloons on the west side of Public Road, and, along with Town Marshal Jack Cassidy, turned them back to the mine—without a shot fired.

Locals praised Sheriff Capp for his fairness during a tense period. Several times in 1910 and 1911, Capp deployed twenty deputies to patrol Lafayette, investigate skirmishes and keep the peace. From 1910 to 1912, Capp made 220 arrests, about one-quarter of which were of union men.

One union miner felt that Capp was sympathetic enough to look the other way when union sympathizers confronted the scabs. "For us, [Capp] was a humanitarian, he'd sympathize with us but there was a lot of things he didn't see," said miner Henry "Welchie" Mathias. "Whenever (the scabs) come up, they'd be getting their pay and they'd head for the saloons. We'd try to roll them, get whatever we could from the bastards. We come up to a saloon, and out this sonofabitch comes with six bottles of beer under each arm and as he got to Dow's [at East Simpson and South Michigan] about six of us nailed that bastard. He had me by the hair, but I was biting him on the leg. We got $70 out of that sonofabitch and we went to Denver for 4th of July. That's more money than we ever knew existed."

THE LATE 1910 AND early 1911 confrontations between scabs and union sympathizers culminated in a nasty dispute that started at 5:00 p.m. on April 15, 1911, involving the Diaz family, strikebreakers who were accused of stabbing to death union member Edwin J. "Ted" Wycherley in front of a local saloon. Wycherley was the UMWA Local 1388's "Door man," an appointed office that was synonymous with a sergeant at arms. On meeting nights, Wycherley checked union cards for those entering the meeting hall and collected dues and fines.

Reported by the *Boulder Daily Camera* as a "murder that was one of the most atrocious in the state's history," the confrontation started at Meikle's Saloon on Saloon Street, now known as Public Road, when words were exchanged between Wycherley and Francisco Diaz and his sons Juan, Manuel and Jose.

Friends of Wycherley who testified at a coroner's inquest said that Francisco Diaz and Wycherley tussled verbally, then Francisco pulled a knife, knocked Wycherley to the ground and stabbed him by "driving the dagger with both hands." Juan Diaz was also implicated in the stabbing, which resulted in Wycherley receiving seven stab wounds, two fatal.

Francisco Diaz, testifying at the coroner's inquest, said that he and his sons had entered the saloon to buy whiskey to take home. After getting their whiskey, the *Boulder Daily Camera* reported that "someone stuck their hand into Francisco's pocket and ask him what he was going to do about it. Someone hit Manuel over the head with a rock, and then Wycherley pulled a gun and shot Juan, who was seriously wounded in the abdomen."

"While the shooting was going on," Francisco said, "everybody crowded around with rocks and we stood in the door for safety. Everyone got around us and pushed us into the street, trying to hit us with rocks."

The Diazes were arrested by Deputy Marshal Jack Cassidy and locked up in the town's seven-foot-by-seven-foot jail cell inside the town hall at Simpson and Harrison.

"News of the murder spread like wildfire," said the published report, and "a crowd gathered around jail demanding the lives of the Mexicans." The crowd tried to break down the back door to the jail with a piece of large drainpipe.

In an effort to keep an armed mob of about five hundred strikers and union sympathizers from lynching the Diazes, Sheriff Capp "went out and, mounting a box where the crowd could see him, made an eloquent plea for the lives of the prisoners."

"I would rather be shot in the road like a dog than to witness this criminal act," shouted the sheriff. "If you must kill someone, kill me."

At dusk, while Capp and local union leader Ed Doyle quelled the riotous crowd, Capp's deputies loaded the Diazes from the jail's back entrance into an escape car owned by *Boulder Daily Camera* editor Alva A. Paddock for transport to the county jail. Capp's automobile was out of service due to a punctured tire. Paddock's role in the affair is not clear, although his newspaper reported that Paddock drove from Boulder to Lafayette "in 23 minutes and arrived with deputy coroner O.C. Ewry."

A sheriff's deputy, with the Diazes on board, drove Paddock's car on a circuitous route back to Boulder via Canfield and Valmont in order to avoid a mob that "had left Louisville to intercept the jail transport."

Funeral services for Wycherley were held on April 20 at Union Hall. Over 1,800 people, including 200 kids let out of school for the occasion, participated in a funeral procession from the hall to the C&S train depot in southeast Lafayette, where Wycherley's remains were loaded for shipment to Cleveland, Utah.

Francisco Diaz (*second from right*) with his sons Jose, Juan and Manuel. *Carnegie Branch Library for Local History, Boulder, Colorado.*

On April 18, a group of four drunken strikebreakers employed at the Industrial Mine in Superior were involved in an old-fashioned Wild West shootout with Deputy Sheriff Ed W. Hockaday. The group of nonunion men were reportedly threatening union officer and Superior town board member Kasper Langgeger. One of the strikebreakers, West Virginia native Grover Mills, drew a sidearm and shot Hockaday in the thigh. The deputy sheriff returned fire and struck Mills in the chest, killing him. That same day, UMWA Lafayette Local 1388 president Ed Doyle wrote in his strike diary that "A strikebreaker passed through town with a large knife in his hand."

At a September 4 gathering of northern Colorado miners at Union Hall, the *Lafayette Leader* reported that State Representative Mike M. Rinn called Wycherley a martyr, saying that he was "attacked and cut to pieces by treacherous Mexicans. He was a toiler in the ranks, a worker. Living honestly and dying honorably for your cause, his life should be a prayer, his death a benediction."

In October 1911, charges against the Diazes were dropped after it was shown that the family had acted in self-defense.

Modern interpretations of the incident have painted the mob's attempt to lynch the Diazes as racially motivated, which is partly true. But tension between striking miners and strikebreakers had reached a breaking point. In his dairy detailing the strike, Ed Doyle wrote that on May 19, 1911, a strikebreaker was arrested for shooting twice at union member George Panisky. Five days prior to the Diaz incident, union sympathizers Richard W. Morgan and Joseph Simpson Jr. were arrested at 11:00 p.m. on April 10 after "a number of shots were fired on Simpson Street," wrote Doyle.

In her book *Latinos of Boulder County, Colorado, 1900–1980*, Marjorie K. McIntosh states that the Diaz incident was "the only mention of a possible lynching in Boulder County, [and] apparently stemmed at least in part from pro-union/anti-scab sentiment."

Tension between strikebreakers and union sympathizers was evident starting the first few weeks of the Long Strike. In over a dozen published accounts of strike violence authored from 1910 to 1914 by ardently pro-union *Lafayette Leader* editor Ira Gwinnup, local miners—most of whom had immigrated decades before from England and Wales—were labeled "union men"; strikebreakers were labeled not by race or skin color, but by country of origin. Russian, Italian, Serbian, Croatian, Mexican, German, Bulgarian, Greek and Slovenian strikebreakers received equal derision from the local media.

The *Boulder Daily Camera*'s anti-union bias would be confirmed in late 1913, when the newspaper's founding publisher, Lucius C. Paddock, coauthored a statewide open letter (at the behest of coal operators) castigating the UMWA and supporting the coal operators' right to hire scabs. In racing from Boulder to Lafayette to cover the 1911 Diaz incident, it was less likely that Lucius's son, Alva Paddock, was concerned about racial injustice and more likely that his motivation was to protect the coal companies' interests.

ON DECEMBER 23, 1910, sixteen union miners, including UMWA Local 1388 president Edward L. Doyle, were arrested in Lafayette and jailed in Denver for violating Judge Whitford's September 1910 court order, which forbade union members from talking with strikebreakers. Whitford maintained that union leaders were guilty of contempt because they'd "beaten up citizens peacefully walking along the street."

Whitford released the union men from jail on February 20, 1911. Several hundred friends greeted the train carrying the released prisoners at the

Lafayette depot, and the Lafayette-Louisville band led a parade up Simpson Street to the town hall.

On June 19, 1911, strikebreaker Albert Crabb was pelted by eggs, and he fingered union men as the culprits. On June 28, Whitford ordered Sheriff Capp to arrest and jail fourteen union men, including Edward Doyle, former president of Local 1388, and three Lafayette town officials, including Lafayette mayor Swan Edison, Lafayette marshal Jack Cassidy and Lafayette night marshal Edwin Jones.

Relying on testimony from strikebreaker and former union member Charles Sherratt, in July 1911, Whitford found the jailed strikers guilty of contempt and sentenced two of them, Edward Doyle and UMWA District 15 secretary William Crawford, to one year in jail. The two were also denied bail. He imposed heavy fines on the other fifteen and committed them to jail "until the fine is paid or until the further order of the court."

In mid-August, a large contingent of Lafayette residents brought picnic baskets to the Denver County Jail and treated the jailed miners to what local newspapers called a "gigantic feast." Treats included ten gallons of ice cream, half a dozen large cakes, pies, salads, thirteen fried chickens, five ducks, four boxes of vegetables and five gallons of sweet milk. The warden and jail guards were invited to partake in the feast. A band was brought along to provide dinner music.

Colorado Supreme Court justice George W. Musser intervened in late August and ordered a stay of execution on the sentences handed down by Whitford. All of the jailed strikers were released.

Elected in November 1912, Colorado governor Elias M. Ammons sent the Colorado militia to Boulder County to quell the strike violence after a September 17, 1913 gun battle raged on the east side of Lafayette. Union sympathizers said that nonunion employees at the Simpson Mine, "the Bulgarians," fired indiscriminately at union members returning from work at an adjacent union mine. The nonunion workers claimed that union sympathizers started the fight by throwing rocks through one of the company buildings in the Simpson compound.

All sides agreed that numerous volleys of gunshots, estimated at over one thousand rounds, originated in both the stockade—shooting toward downtown Lafayette—and in downtown Lafayette—shooting toward the stockade. One person inside the stockade was injured by a gunshot, and one horse was killed.

A law enforcement officer, likely Boulder County sheriff M.P. Capp, displays a confiscated automatic rifle at the Standard Mine east of Lafayette in February 1914 during the United Mine Workers of America strike against the coal companies. A U.S. soldier stands in the background. *Denver Public Library, Western History Collection, X-60586.*

After U.S. troops brought in to referee the strike encamped near the Lafayette cemetery on October 28, 1913, they proceeded to confiscate all guns in Lafayette, even searching homes room-by-room to do so. The following week, children of union men refused to go to school with two boys whose fathers had scabbed the previous summer.

A few weeks later, editors from across the state assembled in Denver to gather facts about the coal strike. In a report of the editors' gathering coauthored by *Boulder Daily Camera* editor Lucius C. Paddock, the group recommended that the miners waive their demand for union recognition, argued that miners were already paid above the national average and stated that "any coal-mine operator has a legal right to employ any person or persons without interference or threats."

The American Fuel Company settled grievances with the miners in March 1912. The company, formed in 1911 when the Mitchell Coal Company and the Economic Coal Company merged, operated the Capitol and Senator mines in addition to six others in the Northern Field. Mary Miller's son J.P. Miller was treasurer for the American Fuel Company.

In the 1912 settlement with the minor operators, local miners received wage concessions and provisions for a union-paid checkweighman, who was charged with observing the coal company's weighing process and reweighing the coal cart if needed. American Fuel gave the miners a three-cents-per-ton increase in pay (not the twelve and a half cents demanded) for removing coal and a five-cents-per-ton increase for pick work, which was the removal of noncoal items such as debris.

The Long Strike was called off by the UMWA in late 1914. The large Colorado coal operators who'd refused all of the miners' demands—Rocky Mountain Fuel Company and Colorado Fuel and Iron—agreed only to rehire the miners who had gone on strike. The general consensus was that the UMWA's 1913–14 statewide strike didn't accomplish much, and it was decades before the union regained its influence in Colorado.

Alva A. Paddock's follow-up reporting in the months after the 1911 near-lynching of the Diazes justifiably included the town's prejudicial treatment of persons of color. This was substantially different than the *Daily Camera*'s earlier coverage of race-related issues in Lafayette. In 1893, Paddock's newspaper advocated that coal miners physically remove from Lafayette anyone of Chinese descent. A February 1893 front-page story congratulated miners for assaulting and chasing away a "Chinaman" who'd arrived in Lafayette "accompanied by his pigtail."

"It is said that some of the Lafayette people object to driving away the Mongolian who recently visited the place," stated Paddock's news story. "We hope there is no truth in it, for of all the foreigners who emigrate to this country, the Chinaman is the least desirable."

Edward Lawrence Doyle (1886–1954), Lafayette resident from 1908 to 1912 and UMWA District 15 secretary-treasurer based in Denver from 1912 to 1917, is better known for his involvement in the fateful 1914 Ludlow Massacre, where he played a key role in communicating to national media the union's perspective of the killings.

As part of that job, he corresponded regularly with labor activist Mother Jones and with author Upton Sinclair, who wrote *King Coal*, an exposé on the dangerous conditions Colorado coal miners faced. Doyle was entrusted by Sinclair to proofread *King Coal* for accuracy prior to its release in 1917.

In 1909, Doyle worked as a checkweighman at the Capitol Mine east of Lafayette, where he advocated for miners' safety, including dogging the mine's owner to remove snow and ice that regularly blocked the mine's escape shaft after snowstorms.

Doyle worked his way into leadership of UMWA Lafayette Local 1388 during the first few years of the 1910–14 Long Strike, organizing the group's picketing and civil disobedience efforts. Doyle aggressively rooted out turncoat union members hired by coal operators to spy on the organization. He also planted two of his own union men, hired from out of state, who posed as scabs in each local coal mine.

9

BREAKING THE BARRIER

The need for skilled coal mine labor brought White midwesterners and European settlers to Lafayette. In the 1920s, the workforce included Japanese and Latino laborers.

WITH LUNCH PAIL IN hand and ready for his shift in the Columbine Mine, coal miner, inventor and Serene coal camp resident Lito Gallegos began the day by dropping his seven-year-old son from his first marriage, Gilbert, at the three-room Serene school. The two walked down the hill along John J. Roche Street, turned right on George T. Peart Street, then walked another half block north along Harry M. Jones Street to the school's front door.

The school was about fifty yards east of the Columbine Mines' main tipple and, as the crow flies, just a few hundred feet from the half duplex that Lito and his wife, Carmella, rented from his employer, Rocky Mountain Fuel Company. The dirt streets were named after company executives, and most company rentals were small, three- or four-room miner's cabins, about six hundred square feet on one level.

Realizing that the available coal in the Simpson Mine in Lafayette was beginning to run out, RM Fuel sank the Columbine shaft in 1914 on the treeless hillside north of today's Highway 7, four miles northeast of Lafayette. In 1926, the Gallegoses were one of about one hundred families living in the sixty-seven cottages and fifteen duplexes inside the isolated, barbed-wire enclosed compound next to the Columbine Mine. The fenced coal camp

Inventor and coal mine supervisor Manuel "Lito" Gallegos, 1922. *Courtesy Tanya Fabian.*

included a school, post office, church, doctor's office, company store, casino, gas station, hotel, movie theater and tennis court.

In addition to the advancements in mechanized coal mining, the increasing usage of the automobile affected Lafayette's labor force. The days when a coal miner could walk to work at the local coal mine were waning. These mines were being replaced by larger, deeper and higher producing regional coal mines such at the Hi-Way, Puritan, Industrial and Columbine. The Simpson Mine closed in 1926, after which a large number of Lafayette coal miners commuted by automobile to mines in Superior, Erie and Frederick. Most of the coal produced by those mines was used at the Valmont electric generation plant in Boulder.

Company employment forms show that Lito Gallegos, who was the holder of several U.S. patents and lived previously in Aguilar, Colorado, could read, write and speak Spanish and English and held state certification as shot firer, shot examiner, fire boss and mine foreman (recognition he received at age nineteen). These were exceptional credentials for a twenty-five-year-old with eleven years of mining experience, including working as mine foreman in RM Fuel coal mines in Las Animas County. RM Fuel's Trinidad and Aguilar-area mines included the Sopris, Tabasco, Primero, Engel and Frederick mines. Lito was hired at the Columbine in April 1926 with the job classification "company work." This meant that Lito was considered a "company man" and would have been given a salary well above the daily $5.25 in wages paid to coal loaders. His job would have included supervisory duties, and he probably would have worked year-round instead of the average 194 days per year that loaders worked.

During the 1920s, the Columbine hired miners of all levels of experience and of every nationality. Employee rolls included recent immigrants from Mexico, Russia, Greece, Bulgaria, Ireland, Italy and Japan. Of the Columbine's four hundred to five hundred workers hired during the 1920s, 52 percent were Latino, almost all of whom were hired as coal loaders, which was the toughest work—shoveling coal into mine cars for eight straight hours. With a few exceptions, such as Lito Gallegos, almost all of the foreign-born workers at the Columbine were hired as loaders, even miners with a decade or more of experience doing skilled labor or supervisory work.

Lito Gallegos probably supervised thirty-seven-year-old Joe Garcia, an immigrant from Mexico who'd also resided in Aguilar and who also held state certification as shot firer, shot examiner and fire boss. Garcia had sixteen years of experience in coal mines, including as driver and timberman. The fifty or so other men that Lito supervised may have included his older brother Jake Gallegos and his father, Alejandro "Alex" Gallegos, both skilled miners who were hired in June 1926 and also lived in the Serene coal camp.

Lito may have supervised his brother-in-law, thirty-one-year-old boxing phenom John Ortega, known as Johnny "Kid Mex," who held the lightweight champion title of the Rocky Mountain region for seven years. John was born in Chihuahua, Mexico, and grew up in Pueblo. He was hired at the Columbine in June 1926 and was married to Mary (Gallegos) Ortega, Lito's sister.

Company employment forms show that about 90 percent of coal miners hired at the Columbine Mine from 1920 to 1929 were fluent in at least two languages. Latino workers, including recent immigrants from Mexico, Jose Camarena, Jesus Casaras and Ben Cabral, could read and speak both English and Spanish. Eastern European immigrants, mostly from Greece, Bulgaria and Russia, spoke English and their native language. Coal loaders Lom Omaye, S.Y. Oh, Henry Okamoto and S. Ogata, immigrants from Japan, spoke Japanese and English.

Lafayette's population in 1900 was nine hundred, and from 1910 to 1950 the population hovered around two thousand residents. The 1900 and 1910 U.S. federal censuses showed a population made up of primarily transplants from the Midwest and immigrants from England, Wales and Ireland. Although a handful of households with Latino surnames—including Jesus Acosta, Lupe Alva, Felix Borago and Miguel Garcia—were listed in the Lafayette section of the 1916 Boulder County Directory, no adults with Latino surnames were listed by the census until 1920. By 1920, Lafayette's population had shifted from mostly White, Anglo-Saxon immigrants to a population that was a mix of native-born residents; Western European immigrants from Spain, England and Ireland; plus Eastern European immigrants and second-generation families from Bohemia, Bulgaria, Greece, Romania, Poland and Lithuania. Twenty-five adults with Latino surnames were listed in the 1920 census, including Colorado and New Mexico natives Felix Cordova, Roque Vigil and Edmond Montoya and Spanish immigrants Joe Munoz, John Rosa and Manuel Minoz. Sixty-nine-year-old Concepcion Mercado, an immigrant from Mexico, is listed as a resident and coal miner, as were Mick Esquivel, Ramarz Agapeto, Margarito Gonzales and Frank Montez. Hipalito Quezada and Phillip Hosa were coal miners renting homes in the Simpson Mine camp.

The majority of immigrants who were counted in the 1920 census had arrived in Lafayette between 1910 and 1916, a period of time that coincided with the Long Strike and coal operators' recruitment of nonunion strikebreakers. During the 1920s, the eastern Colorado sugar beet industry provided nearly twenty thousand seasonal jobs, Colorado railroads employed five thousand Latinos and coal mines employed about three thousand Latinos. Beet workers earned $200 for an entire growing season, while miners could make as much as $200 in a month. Of the Latino workers at the Columbine, 12 percent worked in the beet fields before becoming coal miners.

A June 22, 1917 edition of the *Lafayette Leader* that listed coal miners who contributed to a community fundraiser shows that the Standard Mine, owned starting in 1912 by RM Fuel, was the most integrated of the Lafayette mines. Over 320 miners contributed $1,200 to the Red Cross, an organization that provided battlefield nurses during World War I. Of the four mines represented—Simpson, Mitchell, Standard and Vulcan— the Standard showed seven miners with Latino surnames: G. Castillo, F. Montez, C. Silva, A. Garcia, Albert Cordova, D. Romero and Tony Alvarez. The Simpson Mine had one Latino miner, Frank Martinez.

The 1917 *Lafayette Leader* article noted that "nearly two-thirds of the men [working in the mines] are foreign-born, while nearly the other third are aliens. It is easy to be seen that these foreigners appreciate the freedom of the United States, and they further show by their loyalty at this time that they are going to help maintain that freedom."

UMWA LAFAYETTE LOCAL 1388 meeting minutes show no trace of Latino membership until September 1913. The 1910 U.S. Senate subcommittee report of the racial composition of northern Colorado coal miners, "Immigrants in Industries Part 25," states that Latinos and other persons of color were banned from union membership, but union locals realized during the Long Strike of 1910–14 the necessity of forming labor alliances with native-born and immigrant Latinos. Entering their ten-dollar annual Lafayette Local 1388 dues at the September 25, 1913 meeting were initiates Frank Gonzales, S. Gonzales, F.H. Gallegos, A. Dominguez, Guy Dominguez, Jesus Guzman, Gabriel Vigil, Teofila Tafoya, D. Romero, Ben Martinez, Juan Guerrero and Francisco Guerrero.

Even with expanded membership from Latino miners, the Long Strike crippled the UMWA and left a labor leadership vacuum through the 1920s. Filling the void was the Industrial Workers of the World, also known as the "Wobblies," a radical labor union with a core mission of crushing capitalism. The organization had about 10 percent membership among Colorado coal miners. The IWW called for its membership to strike in October 1927, and six thousand of Colorado's twelve thousand coal miners heeded the call and walked off the job on October 18. The IWW demanded an increase in wages from $5.25 per day to $7.75 per day, an end to workplace discrimination based on age and enforcement of mining laws and safety provisions.

The Columbine continued to operate during the strike and became a magnet for protesting strikers. At the start of the labor dispute, Lito

Gallegos's extended family moved from Serene to Lafayette. Lito's mother, Marguerite, took the kids into town while Mary Ortega packed for the move. Serene Camp management closed the Serene gates, separating Mary from the rest of the family for a short time. During the strike, Lito Gallegos helped evacuate miners' families from Serene.

During the early days of the labor dispute, striking miners picketed at the Columbine and were allowed to peacefully march about four blocks from the north camp entrance, a barbed-wire gate, then through an inner gate to the post office in the general store. On November 21, 1927, about five hundred picketers gathered at the outer north gate and were warned by Weld County deputy sheriff Louis Beynon not to march past the inner camp gate. At the inner gate, protesters were met by plainclothes state police. Tensions escalated to the point where protesters started scaling the locked gate. Police retreated, and the emboldened crowd broke through the gate and surged toward the center of Serene. Waiting about 250 yards ahead were state police, who fired on the approaching crowd. Killed in the fray were miner and Lafayette resident John Eastenes and miners Nick Spanudakhis, Frank Kovich, Rene Jaques, Jerry Davis and Mike Vidovich. Another three dozen people were wounded.

Illustrating the disdain of local unions for the Wobblies, the minutes of UMWA Lafayette Local 1388 from November and December 1927 show no mention of the shooting. Hoping to end the decades-old disputes between coal operators and their employees, RM Fuel president Josephine Roche proposed an equitable and exclusive work contract with the UMWA in May 1928. Over 160 new members joined the UMWA Local 1388 during May and June 1928, nearly doubling the Lafayette local's membership.

10

REMNANTS OF INDUSTRY

Large-scale, factory production of goods and services was confined to Denver, with a few exceptions. But local industry—flour mills, brick factories, coal producers and electrical generating stations—faded quickly.

THE LARGEST PRIVATE-PROPERTY OWNER in the history of Boulder County and the second-largest coal conglomerate west of the Mississippi, Rocky Mountain Fuel Company has its roots in Denver, but Lafayette-area residents and businessmen played a key role in its formation. And there has never been a company that influenced Lafayette's economy more than this coal giant. At the company's peak, about 1915, fully eight in ten of Lafayette's working-age males were either employed by RM Fuel at a local coal mine or were working in a business or industry supporting it.

Founded in the 1870s as Goodridge & Marfell by Henry Goodridge (1832–?) and Erie pioneer Hiram Marfell (1840–1904), both immigrants from England, the coal dealership was incorporated in 1890 as Stewart Coal & Lime Company, located in Denver.

Stewart Coal & Lime Company was purchased in 1893 by the dashing former Nebraska farmer Edgar Edmund Shumway (1862–1914), who launched his coal dealership Shumway & Company in 1891. Shumway's partner in the purchase was Joseph Mitchell Jr. (1847–1921), owner of the New Mitchell Mine in Lafayette. Mitchell's father, Joseph Sr., was the superintendent at the mine and lived in Lafayette.

George Moon and James Sterling Autrey in the grocery and hardware side of the Rocky Mountain Stores Company, 404 East Simpson, about 1920. The retailer was a subsidiary of the Denver-based Rocky Mountain Fuel Company. No coal company offices were in the building. *Lafayette Miners Museum.*

In July 1894, Shumway and Mitchell changed the name of the company from Stewart Coal & Lime Company to Rocky Mountain Fuel Company, operating at 1609 Curtis. Fifteen years later and owning eight southern Colorado and Western Slope coal mines in Rockvale, Sopris, Trinidad, Maitland and Cardiff, E.E. Shumway—sans Joseph Mitchell Jr.—incorporated under the laws of Wyoming as Rocky Mountain Fuel Company of Wyoming in 1910.

In October 1911, RM Fuel purchased the Northern Coal and Coke Company for $5 million from owners F.F. Struby, G.A. Easterly and C.B. Kountze. At the company's peak in 1898, Northern Coal Company executives boasted assets exceeding $30 million. RM Fuel borrowed $1 million and raised another $3.8 million via a bond sale to purchase Northern Coal assets that included 2,500 acres of coal land, nine coal mines, several company stores and Denver coal yards. The mines purchased included the Simpson, Rex, Industrial, Vulcan and Nonpareil mines in Boulder County and the coal rights associated with or formerly held by Empire Coal Company, Aguilar Coal and Mining Company, Louisville Coal Mining Company, Imperial Coal Mining Company and

Union Pacific Coal Company. The sale also included 214 residential lots in Louisville, 25 residential lots in Lafayette, 1,150 pit cars, 80 air-mining machines, 26 horses, 29 wagons and 140 mules.

Company president E.E. Shumway died in 1914 from injuries sustained while investigating the aftermath of the disastrous 1913 explosion that killed thirty-seven miners at the Coryell Vulcan Mine in Garfield County. David W. Brown (1860–1922), who joined RM Fuel in about 1900, succeeded Shumway.

Company financial statements from 1920 show that RM Fuel and its nine-store mercantile division, the Rocky Mountain Stores Company, was managed by D.W. Brown and had over $12 million in assets, $3.5 million in debt and employed 845 people. The company was producing one million tons of coal each year.

John J. Roche (1848–1927), a lawyer and banker by trade, interviewed for a position at Rocky Mountain Fuel Company in 1906, then moved his family from Nebraska to Denver in 1907 to join RM Fuel, replacing company secretary-treasurer H.E. Stewart. Roche eventually became vice-president and treasurer of the company and took over management of RM Fuel after the death of D.W. Brown in June 1922. The largest stockholder in the company, Roche died in 1927 and left an $128,000 estate. That same year, his daughter Josephine Aspinwall Roche (1886–1976) was appointed to the board of directors of RM Fuel. She secured controlling interest in the company in March 1928.

ORGANIZED LABOR, AND THE concept that many workers could leverage a single voice via a labor union, was the most significant shift in the history of paid labor in the United States. And from 1887 through the closing of the local coal mines in the 1940s, Lafayette miners played a major role in the movement.

Although the term *progressivism* wasn't a part of Lafayette's turn-of-the-century lexicon, the average coal miner experienced the daily frustration of an industry that held all the cards. If a miner was shorted on a paycheck due to a discrepancy in the weight of a coal car or was injured or killed in a mine accident, he or his family had no recourse.

The Progressive Party movement gained worldwide attention from 1890 to 1914 and was a social and political response to the Industrial Revolution. The movement was centered on income inequality and the perception that American industry, including the coal operators, had become too powerful.

Josephine Roche. *Author's collection.*

Josephine Roche is considered one of the greatest Colorado advocates for the Progressive cause. Roche started her career in 1912 at the Denver Police Department as inspector of public amusements, an enforcer of the city's curfew laws in the red-light districts and dance halls. Although Roche is often described as being Denver's first policewoman, she was instead the first female police officer in Denver to walk a police beat. She carried a badge but refused to carry a weapon.

In 1913, Roche helped organize the Progressive Service in Colorado, an agency created by the national Progressive Party. She traveled across Colorado, organizing small-town political rallies.

The 1927 shooting of six striking miners by state police and guards at RM Fuel's Columbine Mine, known as the "Columbine Mine Massacre," gave Roche the motivation to acquire 51 percent of the company and set it on a course of sympathizing with, rather than fighting against, its employees.

In 1928, Josephine Roche signed a union contract that some scholars termed the "Industrial Magna Carta." It stipulated an eight-hour workday, allowed miners to elect their own checkweighman, outlined grievance procedures and required the mine to build bathhouses at the coal camp if the miners agreed to pay one dollar per month per man. The agreement with the United Mine Workers of America also stipulated that miners would be paid for dead work, be paid in cash instead of scrip and would no longer be required to live at a coal camp or shop at the company store.

Except for a few years serving as director of the Public Health Service and the National Youth Administration in Franklin D. Roosevelt's administration (1934–37) and as assistant to UMWA leader John L. Lewis (1947–50), Josephine Roche led RM Fuel from 1927 to 1951.

The arrival of a natural-gas pipeline from Texas to Colorado in 1928 and the start of the Great Depression in 1929 was challenging for the coal company. Roche would forego her salary as president of the company and borrowed $680,000 from the UMWA. The company was forced to reorganize in 1944 and was incorporated as a Delaware corporation in 1946.

Most of the mines associated with the bankrupt RM Fuel, including the Columbine, were closed in 1946, after which area mines were owned and run by independent owners. Lafayette's last mine, the Black Diamond, located at today's U.S. 287 and Baseline Road, closed in 1956. The independently owned Hi-Way Mine in Louisville and the Gorham in Superior closed in 1955. Erie's Eagle Mine was the last coal mine to operate in the Northern Coal Field. It closed in 1975.

Still holding valuable land, water rights and mineral rights, RM Fuel experienced a resurgence of sorts in the 1970s under the direction of Gerald "Jerry" R. Armstrong, who was RM Fuel president from 1973 to 2006.

MARY MILLER'S GRANDSONS RALPH Clinton Miller Sr. and Frank Miller mention Mary taking bags of wheat from her road house and stage stop on Rock Creek to be ground into flour at a gristmill "run by a water wheel on Boulder Creek in the white chalk district" at White Rock, northwest of Lafayette.

The Lafayette Feed elevator being built on East Baseline Road, 1955. *Waneka family collection.*

Starting as early as 1859, gristmills were built along Boulder Creek to take advantage of waterpower to turn the heavy grinding stones. The mills east of Boulder City on Boulder Creek included the Valmont Mill (later names included Boulder Valley Mill, Butte Mill and Diamond Mills) northwest of the settlement of Valmont, White Rock Mill near Seventy-Fifth Street and the Canfield Mill near Jasper Road.

As steam power came into fashion around 1890 and water-powered mills became antiquated, flour mills were built closer to rail service.

In 1905–6, Mary Miller helped finance and manage a new flour mill, the Lafayette-Louisville Milling & Grain Company. Her partners for the new venture included James P. Miller, George Bermont, W.A. Burke, William Padfield, John Lipsey, Dr. Horace R. Burns, P.M. Peltier, J.O. Van DeBergh and Denver businessman E.L. Milner, who was the general manager of the mill. It was located on a Burlington railroad spur built for the mill in the 800 block of East Baseline Road, about two hundred feet west of today's Lafayette Feed and Grain elevator.

W.F. Wehman sold his gristmill to Lafayette-Louisville Milling & Grain Company in June 1905, about nine months before the new mill opened.

The Milling & Grain Company flour mill produced its premium brand Silver Tip Flour and operated primarily on electricity provided by the Interurban Power Plant. Mary Miller sponsored a contest to name the premium brand flour in September 1905. The prize was three hundred pounds of flour. Company ledgers show that Silver Tip Flour sold for about twelve cents per pound in 1906 and 1907.

The Lafayette-Louisville Milling & Grain Company mill closed in the 1920s and burned down in 1935.

The town's largest grain elevator, the Lafayette Elevator Company, was built by the Farmer's Union in 1920 adjacent to the C&S tracks at South Public and East Emma. It had a capacity of twenty thousand bushels and was owned by Denver Elevators when it burned down in 1949.

Louis G. Schaaf built the Lafayette Elevator and Milling Company elevator, no longer in operation but known as Lafayette Feed and Grain, in 1955 at 816 East Baseline. That structure still stands.

LAFAYETTE'S FIRST UTILITY FRANCHISE, a twenty-year agreement, was granted by the Lafayette town board to James Cannon Jr.'s Lignite Electric Company in November 1890. Cannon was given authority to "string wire and erect poles or posts" in town rights-of-way, but no work was done.

Workers gather outside the Interurban Power Plant, built in 1906 by the Western Power Light Company. *Lafayette Public Library*.

A subsequent attempt to bring electricity to Lafayette was reported in the *Boulder Daily Camera* in 1892. E.B. Light, owner of the Denver Manufacturing Company in Denver and the Baker Mine on Blue Ribbon Hill east of Lafayette, wanted to build an electrical grid from north Denver to Coal Park, east of Lafayette. In late 1892, Lafayette town trustees Dr. J.H. Couch and C.C. Rosenbaum visited Light in Denver to encourage his enterprise. Boulder residents invited Light to Boulder to discuss extending the line another twelve miles from Lafayette to Boulder.

In 1895, Mary Miller leased a small piece of land on the C&S railroad spur just west of the Spencer-Simpson Mine to John S. Spencer, who incorporated the Lafayette Machine Electric Light & Power Company. The town had granted Spencer a forty-year franchise a year earlier. Spencer's coal-fired plant, funded by a loan from Miller, generated a twelve-volt direct current from dusk until midnight. Primarily used to power the town's nine streetlights, only a handful of Lafayette and Louisville homes were wired.

Machine Electric Light steam boilers relied on surface wells for water, a supply that started to dwindle as coal mining displaced more and more aquifers. Lack of water resulted in the power plant closing, after which James Cannon Jr. stepped in and bought the plant for his brother Edmund M. "Ed" Cannon. The Cannons secured both coal and water for the steam plant from the nearby Simpson Mine. But James Cannon Jr.'s United Coal Company began to disintegrate in 1896, and the Simpson Mine water supply to his brother's power plant was cut. Ed Cannon unplugged the power plant in the summer of 1898 and told the town board that "a great many did not feel able to pay for lights at present."

As James Cannon Jr.'s next enterprise, Northern Coal Company, took shape, investors H.E. Becker, Jack Carreuthers and James Simpson Jr. (John H. Simpson's brother) took over Cannon's failing power plant and incorporated as the Lafayette-Louisville Electric Company in late 1898. The company's intent was to first supply electricity to the coal mines, then offer it to local residents. Becker, Carreuthers and Simpson sold to Northern Colorado Power Company in 1902.

Simultaneous to the formation of the Lafayette-Louisville Electric Company, a James Cannon Jr. shell company, the Rocky Mountain Power Company, was formed in 1898 in partnership with E.E. Shumway. A July 1, 1898 *Denver Times* article reported that the company intended to supply electricity to metalliferous mines in Boulder, Gilpin and Clear Creek Counties and coal mines in northern Colorado. Plans were made for a two-thousand-horsepower steam plant near Lafayette that would be located adjacent to a proposed coal mine. The newspaper report said that the plant was to be in operation by November 1898.

As was the case with other enterprises formulated by James Cannon Jr., the newspaper said "a list of names, purporting to be the list of incorporators, was filed with the articles, but it develops that these names are being used simply as dummies to divert attention from the backers of the scheme, who do not desire their names known." The articles of incorporation were prepared by Northern Coal attorney Charles T. Brown, and the "dummy" incorporators included Minn S. Page, J.G. O'Bryan, C.B. Rich and R.C. Bogy.

Rocky Mountain Power Company's plans fell through, but the Northern Colorado Power Company came along a few years later and began construction of the six-thousand-kilowatt Northern Colorado and Interurban Power Plant in 1906. It supplied alternating current to the electric-powered Interurban passenger trolley service that connected

Boulder to Denver. Joseph J. Henry of Denver developed the business plan and directors included W.F. Crossley, Tyson Dines, W.H. Allison, Senator F.E. Warren (from Wyoming), William J. Barker, Thomas Kelly, Robert S. Ellison, William Mayer and C.C. Bromley.

Blue Ribbon Hill east of Lafayette was initially thought to be the best place for the new electric plant, due to the presence of Coal Creek water. The power plant was instead located on the south edge of what is now Waneka Lake. Boulder County Clerk records show that Mary Miller bought the reservoir in 1904 from William, Frank and Guy Harmon, but the Harmons retained rights to some of the water flowing into Miller and Harmon Reservoir.

Northern Power documents from 1906 and reservoir records at the Colorado Division of Water Resources both show that the original name of Waneka Lake was "Henry Waneka No. 1 Reservoir." State records indicate that the lake was built by Adolf Waneka in 1865 to hold water coming out of a nearby spring. Adolf gave his interest in the lake to his son Henry "Boye" Waneka, who then sold to William, Frank and Guy Harmon in 1897. Northern Power expanded the lake, which was later called Plant Lake, in 1906 to store twenty-eight million cubic feet of water for its steam generators.

Alternating current electric lights started to be switched on in Lafayette homes in about 1907. Alternating current lights were also installed in coal mine tunnels, and electric-powered trams began to operate in local mine haulageways. Mules were still used to haul coal from the coal face to the haulageway.

Among the first successful central generation and power distribution systems in the country, the Interurban Power Plant supplied power to Lafayette, Louisville, Longmont, Loveland, Fort Collins, Boulder and most of northern Colorado, including coal mines and sugar beet factories. Northern Power changed its name to Western Light and Power in 1914 and was acquired by the Public Service Company in 1923. After the Valmont electric generation plant was built near Boulder in 1924, Lafayette's Interurban Power Plant was used on a standby basis. It last operated in 1948 and was torn down in the 1950s.

A DENVER PHOTOGRAPHER HIRED by the Mountain States Telephone and Telegraph Company in 1914 to document telephone lines running through Lafayette captured a seemingly ordinary image at the corner of what is today's 111th Street and Baseline Road. The image shows the tiers of pole wires that formed the nation's first transcontinental phone line, a communication backbone running from San Francisco to New York that came north from Denver and followed the old Cherokee Trail route to Laramie, Wyoming.

The image also shows the town of Lafayette's riveted-steel water storage standpipe, located at the time just north of the intersection of Geneseo Street and Bermont Avenue. The standpipe was built around 1907, was about twenty feet in diameter and ninety feet tall and held over 150,000 gallons of water. In 1906, town trustees were concerned about the potential of subsidence and negotiated an agreement with Northern Coal and Coke Company, owners of the Simpson Mine, that coal under the standpipe be left in place.

The coal company was compensated for the coal that wasn't removed.

Along with showing state-of-the-art technology for 1914, the accompanying image of the nation's first transcontinental phone line

A 1914 photo from the Mountain States Telephone and Telegraph Company looking south from 111th Street toward Baseline Road shows the nation's first transcontinental phone line passing through Lafayette. *History Colorado, CHS.X7446.*

Clipped poles from the transcontinental phone line remain along North 111th Street in Lafayette, 2020. *Photograph by the author.*

passing through Lafayette shows a speed-limit sign that reads: "Speed Limit for Autos Motors Is 8 Miles" and a woman at lower right hanging clothes in her side yard.

Also visible at lower right is an auto repair shop that was advertising car tires.

11

A DARK PERIOD COMES TO LIGHT

For twelve years, the Ku Klux Klan dominated Lafayette politics and spread fear and hate as the hooded menace targeted Latinos and Catholics.

JULY FOURTH CELEBRATIONS IN Lafayette's early years involved picnics, a baseball game at city park followed by ice cream and an evening capped with a grand ball at the Union Hall. But the night of July 4, 1923, was different.

A half mile east of town above the Standard Mine, high along the ridge known as Blue Ribbon Hill, the night sky was lit by a burning cross. It was both a ritual and a message.

The message, visible to all townspeople, was that the Ku Klux Klan had formally organized in the community and that thirty-one new members of Lafayette Klavern, Chapter 22, had sworn to uphold the racist edicts of the Invisible Empire.

A burning cross was a tool of intimidation and often preceded violent acts by the KKK and was used to celebrate lynchings of African Americans. The burning of the cross has Scottish influences. One theory says that the KKK, founded in 1866 in Tennessee, patterned the ritual after Scottish soldiers who in the Middle Ages used burning crosses as rallying symbols. Another says that crosses were set afire on Scottish hilltops to warn of enemy invasion.

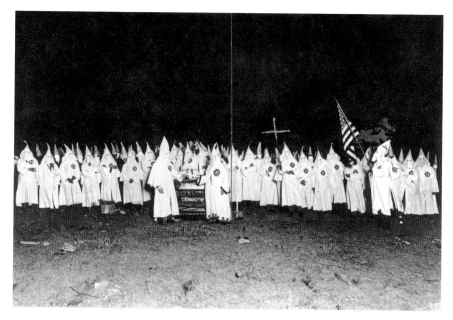

Klu Klux Klan members from Lafayette assembled with five hundred fellow regional Klansmen in a canyon near Boulder, 1925. *Denver Public Library, Western History Collection, Z-188.*

The July 13, 1923 *Lafayette Leader* reported that the Boulder lodge of the Ku Klux Klan directed the Blue Ribbon Hill initiation and that "many more from Lafayette will soon be enrolled as members of the order."

Thus unfolded Lafayette's darkest period, from 1923 to 1935, which was filled with hate and racism veiled by the KKK's outward claims of wholesome values, virtuousness and temperance.

Nationally, the KKK targeted African Americans and Jews; the local chapter targeted Latinos, Eastern Europeans and Catholics in Louisville and Lafayette. Latino residents were especially vulnerable, because the hate group assumed they were both Catholics and immigrants to the United States.

One Weld County resident found turn-of-the-century Lafayette fertile ground for White supremacist ideology. Nationally renowned White supremacist, Pillar of Fire founder and KKK supporter Bishop Alma Bridwell White lived in Erie for several years and preached the Louisville-Erie-Broomfield-Lafayette circuit in the 1890s. An advocate for women's rights and a prohibitionist, White was also an anti-Semite who encouraged her circa 1909 Pillar of Fire male parishioners to wear uniforms that the *Leadville Herald Democrat* described as "blue jumper coats, knee breeches, leather leggings and police-like helmets."

In addition to helping launch the Lafayette Methodist Church between 1894 and 1897, Alma Bridwell White tutored her family in the liturgy of hate. Her brother C.W. Bridwell held Lafayette revival meetings starting in 1916 at a former Public Road saloon and was the featured speaker at a 1925 Klan recruiting rally at Union Hall. The Pillar of Fire Church also operated a missionary on East Simpson Street and owned the Baseline Road and Harrison Avenue property where the 1940s-era Methodist church was built.

The national rise of the Ku Klux Klan after 1900 has been attributed in part to the glamorized representation of the KKK in the 1915 motion picture *The Birth of a Nation*, which debuted in Denver in July 1916. A front-page article in the *Lafayette Leader* promoting the Denver premiere said "the play shows the formation of the Ku Klux Klan, which was organized secretly to control the negroes, who, after the war, had become imbued through the artifices of the Northern politicians with the idea that they were to govern those who before had been their masters."

D.W. Griffith's *The Birth of a Nation* premiered at the Jewel Theater in Lafayette on October 25, 1916. The newspaper dramatically promoted the film by saying it would "force you to grasp the back of the seat in front of you until your fingers ache and then relax them as some touching, tender scene appears."

In addition to the cross burning at the group's launching in 1923, three other publicized cross burnings included New Year's Eve on December 31, 1923, when the group burned a cross at Public Road and Simpson Street. The *Lafayette Leader* reported the downtown cross burning as an offering of "good cheer."

About two years later, in an incident retold by Lafayette residents John James and Florence Farris, the KKK burned a cross in the front yard at 306 East Cannon Street, the home of Joseph Welter. A Catholic and naturalized citizen who'd immigrated from Germany in 1880, Welter was also a former Lafayette town board member who ran for office on the Taxpayers ticket.

In 1934, a cross was burned on the front yard of 304 East Chester Street, the home of Santiago and Rose Lueras. Scores of other cross burnings took place in Lafayette and Louisville, with the Catholic church in Lafayette being a frequent target.

Estimates over the years have put Lafayette's KKK membership at one hundred to two hundred members, an estimate based on participants when the group held formal parades. One such parade took place prior to a fall 1925 Lafayette Klavern meeting at the Odd Fellows Hall on East Simpson Street. "Delegates were present from Longmont, Denver and other surrounding towns," said the story in the October 23, 1925 *Lafayette Leader*. "In full regalia and preceded by a cavalcade of horsemen and a Denver band, a procession was formed which marched through the streets."

Although billed as a secret organization, local KKK parade participants on horse mount revealed their identities. William Lafayette "Fay" Miller, Mary Miller's grandson, "led the parade [dressed in a KKK robe and hood] because he had this beautiful white horse," said Faye's nephew Ralph Clinton Miller in a 1988 oral history interview. "Everyone knew it was him."

Lafayette KKK members included teachers, mayors, town board members, coal miners, fire department volunteers, town employees, mailmen, newspaper editors, lawyers, ministers, shopkeepers and descendants of Lafayette's town founder.

In the mid-1920s, the nationwide count of KKK members exceeded four million. The Colorado Ku Klux Klan membership roll preserved in the archives of History Colorado in Denver show that the Invisible Empire's 1924–28 statewide membership totaled 47,802. The Colorado Chapter of the Women of the Ku Klux Klan had thirty-five Klaverns and 11,000 members in 1924 and 1925. Primary residences of male membership were concentrated in Denver and Edgewater but included several Front Range communities—Pueblo, Golden, Fort Collins and Lafayette. The 1920s KKK roster was donated to the Colorado Historical Society in 1936 with the condition that it not be made public until 1990.

Lafayette residents who paid ten dollars to be registered Ku Klux Klan members included Carl Tyner (no. 6756), Joseph Wm. Holliday (no. 7651), Grover C. Nixon (no. 9210), Ray Burt (no. 10028), Richard Saunders Jr. (no. 10029), Fred Van Arsdale (no. 11170) and Logan J. Ross (no. 11171). There were probably more from Lafayette registered, but the KKK collection is missing records 26,185 through 46,001.

Logan Ross was a World War I veteran and a teacher at Lafayette High School. He was elected to the Lafayette town board on the Citizens ticket in 1930 along with fellow KKK member Lee Baker. Ross gave up his seat on the council in 1934 after being elected the secretary of the Lafayette District 52 School Board.

When asked in 1926 whether the KKK had infiltrated Lafayette's school faculty, which was mostly women and numbered about twenty-four people for grades one through twelve, Principal W.A. Morrison told the *Lafayette Leader* that he was "denying statements that there was a discrimination between Catholics and Protestants or that all of the teachers of the Lafayette schools had to be members of the KKK." Morrison made a weak defense of the last accusation by saying that "he was not [part of the KKK], that three other men were not and that one woman teacher was openly opposed to the Klan." Doing basic subtraction meant that many faculty members were.

This was supported by regular visits to Lafayette by Boulder KKK advocate Dr. Charles Brown, a professor at the University of Colorado who was an accreditation expert, at the time known as a high school inspector. Brown was a featured speaker at a December 1923 KKK rally at Lafayette's Union Hall, located at the corner of East Simpson Street and Gough Avenue. According to the *Lafayette Leader*, Brown gave "an outline of the objects and purposes of the organization…and a clear-cut exposition of the principles of the Klan." In 1925, Brown was a featured speaker at the late October dedication of the newly constructed Lafayette High School.

One of Lafayette's most revered citizens from 1930 to the early 1970s was Merrill Angevine, the school district's superintendent starting in 1934. Angevine was more forceful than previous administrators in seeing that local Latinos were represented in the school's choirs, theater productions and sports teams. At the same time, there is evidence that he acquiesced to the racist leanings of the school's Parent Teacher Association, which in 1935 was an all-White volunteer organization composed of spouses of local KKK leaders. Mrs. Ray Burt was the group's president.

Lafayette's racist roots can be traced back to the early White coal miners, who refused to work alongside persons of color. During pre-1900 northern Colorado coal strikes, the threat of bringing Black strikebreakers from Denver was used as leverage in contract negotiations with the all-White labor unions.

"President [James] Cannon of the coal company says that if the men who were persuaded not to go to work tomorrow [because of the strike] do not return there will be others that he can get. But he says he does not intend importing any negroes as was rumored," stated the August 2, 1898 *Denver Republican* newspaper.

Those racial barriers were broken in 1910, when the coal operators recruited Mexican and southern Colorado Latino coal miners to Lafayette to replace the union miners on strike. This is evidenced by the documented presence and growth in the Latino population after the 1910 federal census. But that doesn't mean that Lafayette and surrounding areas were void of Latinos prior to 1910.

Crime stories published in the local newspapers from 1900 to 1910—and always casting Latinos in a negative light—show Latino residents living near Waneka Lake and living and working on area farms. And, according to federal labor records, a few worked in area coal mines. But anyone of color in the town proper faced open racism. A May 20, 1905 news item in the *Lafayette News* stated that "four full-blooded Mexicans passed through town Friday morning. It would have been a good time for someone to make a rep"—either chasing away or harassing the Latinos would have netted the White harasser hero status.

The KKK, which held power at Lafayette city hall for most of the 1920s and 1930s, won the town's mayoral seat in 1924. Local Klavern leader Lee Baker was elected mayor on the Citizens ticket along with at least three other Klansmen. After being dormant for five years, the Citizens political party was reconstituted in 1922, one year after the death of Mary Miller. Formed in the late 1890s by Miller, the anti-saloon Citizens ticket fought to keep Lafayette a dry town. The competing political party, the pro-saloon Taxpayers ticket, advocated for limited liquor sales on the west side of Public Road.

It's not by chance that the reconstituted Citizens Party coincided with the formation of the Lafayette Klavern in 1923. Evidence strongly suggests that membership of the Ku Klux Klan, the Citizens political party, the volunteer fire department and the Lafayette town board overlapped.

Even though Baker didn't run for reelection in 1926, he stayed in office after non-Klansman Dr. V.W. Porter of the Taxpayers party backed out. Porter is better known in town history as the person that single-handedly navigated Lafayette through the 1918 Spanish flu pandemic. In the April 1926 mayoral election, Porter beat Citizens ticket candidate Frank Miller. According to the *Lafayette Leader*, Porter didn't take office in 1926, because he "did not care for the honor" and declined to be sworn in. Porter never gave an explanation for the change of mind.

Laws at the time stated that a mayor had to remain in office until his or her successor was sworn in. This meant that Lee Baker and the KKK, perhaps through intimidation of Dr. Porter, held on to the seat of power.

Local KKK influence also extended into the area's largest employer, the Columbine Mine, located four miles northeast of Lafayette, and the Standard Mine, located northeast of Lafayette. Management of both mines were members of either the Erie or Lafayette Klaverns, meaning that Klan brethren were given preference in filling jobs.

Without a doubt, the KKK also influenced coverage in the local newspaper, the *Lafayette Leader*. In the 1920s, the heyday of the Lafayette Klavern of the Ku Klux Klan, no reporting of Klan activities was cast in a negative light except a story about the Klan donating a U.S. flag to the town board in 1922. The editor of the *Leader*, B.J. Radford, described the nighttime folly of Klansmen not being able to shimmy up the flagpole at city hall to place the flag. Town employee Guy Gordon was tasked with placing the flag the next morning and did so easily and "with the dexterity of a squirrel."

Although there's no direct evidence that Radford belonged to the KKK, he published details of Klan visits to several local churches that would have been hard to obtain without being present. Frequent trips to Boulder and Longmont to hear state and national leaders of the KKK speak were reported firsthand by Radford, and after known Klavern leader Lee Baker was elected Lafayette town mayor in 1924, Baker appointed Radford as town magistrate (judge).

Mention of Latino residents was also sparse in the *Lafayette Leader* between 1920 and 1933. Lafayette and surrounding agricultural areas had about two thousand residents and about one hundred residents with Latino surnames, according to the 1920 federal census. Lafayette residents with surnames such as Borrego, Silva, Abeyta, Manzanares, Montez, Garcia and Romero weren't mentioned in news columns more than a handful of times, mostly making the school enrollment updates provided by the local District 52 office. Students Sandy and Ambrose Garcia were mentioned, as were Manuel, Gilbert, Eleanor and Sam Abeyta and Lupie and Genevieve Ortega. Lucy Martinez and Richard Vigil also made the newspaper's pages. In news from the local churches, parishioner David Lueras Jr. is mentioned for a leadership role in the Baptist youth fellowship.

In reporting crime committed by Latinos, which made the front page, anyone with a Latino surname was derogatorily labeled in the newspaper as a "Mexican." Radford, the newspaper editor/town judge, made sure that court hearings involving Latinos were fully reported, which rarely happened when criminal defendants were White.

Radford died suddenly in October 1926, and his wife, Edith L. Radford, published the paper until February 1929, when Emil G. Sands took over.

THERE ARE TWO VERSIONS of the 1920s hazing of the editor of the *Lafayette Leader* by the Ku Klux Klan.

In one version, which takes place around 1925, the local newspaper editor was spying on a local KKK meeting "at the Wilcox Dairy Farm" and, after being discovered, was taken to Blue Ribbon Hill and threatened at knifepoint in front of a burning cross. The unattributed version of the story was published first in a 1981 *Lafayette News* article, then retold in the 1990 book *Lafayette, Colorado History: Treeless Plain to Thriving City*.

This version is backed by the local KKK's public criticism of Radford in 1925 editions of the Boulder-based *Rocky Mountain American*, a sanctioned publication of the Ku Klux Klan. In consecutive editions, the Klan correspondent based in Lafayette accuses Radford of being "anti-education," because Radford questioned the high cost of building the new high school.

"It certainly seems a pity that a community like Lafayette who has a statewide reputation for the size, spirit and quality of its Klan has to have such narrow minded people to put out its public newspaper," wrote the Klan correspondent.

In 1975, coal miner Welchie Mathias, then eighty-one years old, said that the KKK instead "chased Sands that ran the *Lafayette Leader*; they rode him on a rail and all that kind of stuff." In 1978, old-timer Boughton Noble said that Emil G. Sands "put an editorial in his paper concerning the movement. They took him out east of Lafayette to Blue Ribbon Hill and I guess they really gave him the worst. I guess he became scared to death and hysterical." Other mentions of the kidnapping/hazing/encounter describe the Klan as wanting to "tar and feather" Sands.

As stated previously, there's no remaining evidence of ill will directly expressed about the KKK or any challenge to the group by the local newspaper. That being said, there are editions missing from the newspaper's archives. Several archived editions have front-page stories neatly cut out, leaving a hole. So, it's possible that Radford and Sands, both Protestants, directly repudiated the KKK, but no written evidence remains.

So, how did Emil G. Sands get crosswise with the KKK?

From 1924 to 1927, the KKK gained significant political power in town, city, county and state governments. KKK members successfully (and equally) infiltrated the Democrat and Republican Parties. The KKK's political influence began to decline starting in 1925, when the state KKK grand dragon John Galen Locke was indicted for tax evasion. In 1927, Governor Clarence Morley, a KKK member, decided not to seek reelection.

But vestiges of the secret group remained for many years in elected positions throughout Colorado, including Lafayette.

After taking ownership of the *Leader* in 1929, Emil Sands began publishing an anonymous front-page gossip column, Town Tattle, under the pen name "Heck," who was interested in "a bigger and better Whoopee." It featured mostly innocuous observations about love interests and courtships occurring at local dances and get-togethers. Sometimes, names were revealed; sometimes, they weren't.

In April, Heck revealed that a "big, bad, bald man was simply slaying the heart of a dear, sweet school teacher." We don't know who the bad man was, but Sands' Town Tattle columns were apparently taken a bit too personally. After broaching the fine line of Lafayette's secret underpinnings, and three months into the column, Heck announced that he'd be leaving town on an extended vacation.

A few months later, Sands launched another anonymous column, Reflections, written by "Sub-Rosa" (which means "under the rose" or "secret" in Latin). The column openly attacked the missteps of town leaders, mostly KKK members, which had not occurred in the newspaper prior to Sands's ownership.

In early August 1929, Sub-Rosa openly criticized the town board for not fixing the town's streets and sidewalks and took the board to task for buying a "toy roller" to compact and smooth out the town's dirt streets. Without explanation, the anonymous column ceased after the August 23 edition.

Again, the exact dates of the KKK kidnapping of Sands is not known, but the sudden starting and stopping of the grating newspaper columns may be an indication that Lafayette's underworld had become highly irritated.

ESTABLISHED IN 1905, THE St. Ida Church of the Immaculate Conception in Lafayette was among several local churches converted to hospitals during the 1918 Spanish flu pandemic. The church contributed in many ways in helping early Lafayette survive and prosper. Its Catholic parishioners were numerous and composed largely of Latinos and Eastern Europeans who'd moved to Lafayette to mine coal.

In perusing the archived weekly editions of the *Lafayette Leader* from 1920 to 1933, a reader will find scant mention of St. Ida Church. There were a dozen or so mentions of the church in local death notices, but otherwise almost no evidence (in the newspaper, at least) that the church existed.

Conversely, the town's Protestant Christian churches—Baptist, Methodist (Methodist Episcopal, or M.E.), Congregational, Nazarene and Christian Science—received prominent write-ups on the front page, with both a schedule of upcoming services and a wrap-up of the previous week's services. The newspaper's front-page Easter and Christmas messages to the community were always penned by a Protestant minister. And the auxiliary support groups of the local Protestant churches, usually referred to as ladies aid societies, received as much publicity as they wanted.

The intertwining of the Ku Klux Klan and the Protestant churches received spectacular coverage. On the numerous occasions that members of the white-robed Klavern visited church services, the visits were glowingly reported.

On January 11, 1925, the Methodist church services included the Knights of the Ku Klux Klan, who brought a guest lecturer and their own string orchestra and choir. The newspaper reported that "preceding the address about 150 members of the Klan and American Crusaders, wearing their hoods and gowns, entered the side door of the hall and marched across the front of the room and down the aisle to the back of the room where they stood during the remainder of the meeting. As they passed the stage each one dropped into the contribution box a coin. The sum of the money realized was $102.50. This added to the $57 contributed by the congregation was turned over to the building fund of the M.E. church."

The following Sunday, Reverend J.C.B. Hopkins told his Methodist parishioners that he was "grateful for their [the KKK's] monetary offering, but the promise of moral support of the hooded knights was by far more precious and encouraging." Hopkins went on to say that "unless he received the support of the church people and right-thinking citizens of Lafayette in the work he was trying to do, he was ready to join the Klan and work with them."

On March 19, 1926, it was reported that about seventy hooded members of the local KKK and their spouses entered the Methodist church auditorium singing "Onward, Christian Soldiers." Each member of the group filed past the pulpit and dropped a coin into the collection box before marching to the Baptist church in west Lafayette to repeat the process.

The repeated, formal visits by the KKK to the Methodist, Baptist and Congregational churches were reported in the newspaper over about a five-year period. Of all the ministers, J.C.B. Hopkins seemed most appreciative, because the Klan's monetary contributions, over $300, were used to renovate the Methodist church building at Gough Avenue and Geneseo Street, which had been damaged by fire in 1924.

A reemergence of the Lafayette Klavern took place in 1934, when a volunteer effort to build a town swimming pool was usurped by the KKK. Townspeople had been promoting for years the idea of a sand-bottom swimming pool to be located at the city park adjacent to the cemetery at Public Road and Baseline Road. The Union Pacific deeded twenty acres for the cemetery and park in 1907, and initial plans for the park included a half- mile track for horse racing.

Starting on August 11, 1933, requests for bagged cement donations went out in the *Lafayette Leader*, and a weekly tally of donations was published. In about four weeks, Lafayette townspeople, churches, community groups and businesses donated 131 sacks out of an estimated 300 needed to build the pool.

Most individuals donated just one or two sacks. The largest donation by an individual, ten sacks at about seventy cents per bag, was made the week of August 11 by E. Emma Street homeowner and coal mine fire boss David H. Lueras on behalf of the Lueras family, which included his nephew Santiago Lueras, also a coal miner. Santiago and his wife, Rose (Lovato) Lueras, owned a house on East Chester Street.

Intimidation and harassment of the Luerases by local KKK members occurred immediately after the publication of the donation list. On August 15, David (D.H.) Lueras placed a public notice in the *Lafayette Leader* stating that "anyone trying to break into my garage or property will meet with a serious accident. I will not be responsible for what happens."

Work on the pool stalled, but in early 1934, the Works Progress Administration stepped in to complete the pool and contributed four hundred sacks of cement. WPA was a federal program to provide jobs during the Great Depression. The pool was completed in late spring 1934, about the same time that the town board decided to turn over operation of the pool to the Lafayette Fire Department, led by Chief Harry Crews and fire board president Rufus Griffith. No reason was given for the move, but the fire department later claimed that it was tasked with obtaining all the equipment—through donations—for the pool. The town, it said, couldn't afford to take on those expenses.

Years later, Clifford Alderson, who was a member of the town board at the time, said the town leased the pool to the fire department to get the town "off the hook." Alderson told the *Lafayette News* in 1989 that "people weren't mixing quite as well as they do now and there was some question as to who should swim in the pool."

Holdovers from peak KKK activity in the mid-1920s carried over into the 1930s, especially in the volunteer fire department and in city hall. In the

April 1934 town election, the mayor, Harry Grief, and five of the six town board members elected—James Berry, Ralph Kemp, Ted Lumley, Clifford Alderson and William Lewis—ran on the Citizens ticket, which had a ten-year alliance with and connection to the KKK. The sixth board member, Joe Mathias, who was a member of the Lafayette Fire Department, was elected on the (non-KKK aligned) Taxpayers ticket.

When the Lafayette pool opened in the summer of 1934, a fire department subcommittee placed a twenty-inch-by-thirty-inch sign, painted by volunteer firefighter Henry Mathias, at the entry stating "Firemen's Pool. We reserve the right to reject any person with cause. White trade only. Lafayette Fire Department." On July 31, Rose Lueras and her daughter were denied entry to the pool. Other residents turned away included Tobias Gomez, Eddie Abeyta, Don Tafoya, Fred Vigil and Fred Montoya.

Rose Lueras filed a lawsuit in the Boulder District Court on August 11 claiming that the town of Lafayette and the Lafayette Fire Department conspired to "deny their right to use" the pool, a violation of the Treaty of Guadalupe Hidalgo, the Fourteenth Amendment of the U.S. Constitution and civil rights statutes of Colorado. Parties to the lawsuit included Gregorio Roybal, George Roybal, Sam Roybal, Tobias Gomez, Fred Montoya, John Lueras, D.H. Lueras, D.C. Lueras, Santiago Lueras, Abe Abeyta, Eddie Abeyta, Tony Sisneros. L.B. Rodriguez, Mrs. Valdez, Mr. Gillen, Cruz Gallegos, John Ortega, Jose Trujillo, Roberto Chavez, David Salazar, Louis Manzanares, Joe Manzanares, Bill Manzanares, Louis Chavez, Jose Tafoya, Don Tafoya, Ramon Pena, Levi Rivera, Garfield Borrego, Jose Medrano, Pablo Rivera, Eliseo Fernandez and Fred Vigil.

The hooded menace reemerged a few weeks later, when local KKK members marched through most of Old Town, starting at city park with two burning crosses, then winding their way through streets east of Public Road. Klan members stopped periodically at intersections to sing Klan songs.

Not surprisingly, the *Lafayette Leader* reported very little about the conflict. Any reporting that the newspaper did was lost when the August 3, 1934 edition of the newspaper went missing (and is no longer in the archives). The August 31, 1934 edition also vanished.

To escape harassment, in early 1935, Rose Lueras moved to Santa Monica, California. In June 1935, she was killed in an auto accident. Judge Claude C. Coffin of the Boulder District Court convened the case a few months later, and Rose's thirteen-year-old daughter, Rosebelle, was substituted as the lead petitioner.

Santiago and Rose Lueras. *Courtesy Frank Archuleta.*

Coffin dismissed the lawsuit, arguing that the petitioners mention the offensive "White trade only" sign in their court filings but didn't use it as the basis of their complaint of discrimination. He also pointed to evidence in court filings that the pool was not open when some of the petitioners claimed they were barred from using it. Lastly, Coffin wrote that the city leasing the pool to the fire department wasn't a conspiracy to exclude Latinos and that "the expression of denial didn't come from any of the defendants or the representatives of any of them."

In 1937, the Colorado Supreme Court affirmed the lower court decision, which hinted at the proper route for an appeal, namely that specific violations of Colorado civil rights laws should be cited. But by then it was too late.

Although the outdoor pool remained open in the summer of 1934 and the CWA completed the pool's bathhouse, it closed that fall and never reopened. In May 1936, it was filled in, and no trace of it remains. In 1937, Colorado Supreme Court justice Haslett Burke said in affirming the district court dismissal that it was unwise to discriminate against anyone based on race or color. "We are disposed to emphasize the thoughtful suggestion of the [district] trial judge that race and color should not be made the basis of discrimination," said Burke. "It tends to induce ill feelings—always detrimental to the well-being of society."

Information about the Klan's influence in Lafayette is hard to come by, because of the prominent names associated with the group. In the local newspaper, in local history books and in recorded narratives made in the 1970s and 1980s, very little discussion of the Ku Klux Klan takes place. Other than a 1990 oral history given by Sally Martinez (1917–2000), there's minimal repudiation of the KKK, few members were named and knowledge of the group's activities came from "a friend who belonged."

Details of the extensive local influence and racism of the Klan was brought to light after Percy and Carolyn Conarroe began publishing local history pieces in 1974 in their startup *Lafayette News* newspaper. A story about the Klan was published by the *News* in 1981 and again in 1989, when construction of the city's indoor swimming pool uncovered concrete remnants of the old outdoor pool.

In 2019, longtime resident Frank Archuleta researched and documented the 1934 swimming pool incident, including the mistreatment of the Luerases and decades-long discrimination against Latino families. In 2019, the City of Lafayette issued a formal apology and named the indoor pool at the Bob Burger Recreation Center the "Rose Lueras Pool."

12

SUSTAINING A COMMUNITY

M exico land grant settlers in southern Colorado, with ties to Lafayette families, set the stage for today's irrigation methods and water rights.

FELIZ DE JESUS BORREGO worked dutifully each summer in the early 1850s to clear and maintain the irrigation ditches running through his farmland in the San Luis Valley, water used to grow crops and maintain livestock in an arid climate. The ditches near today's San Luis, Colorado, known as "acequias" in Spanish, were first used in the southwest areas of Colorado three hundred years before Feliz and his wife, Juanita, settled there. The ditches were hand dug starting at Culebra Creek then expanded by wooden plow pulled by horse.

Land along the acequias was divided into narrow strips, each one hundred veras (one hundred yards) wide. The narrow strip perpendicular to the irrigation ditch could be up to twenty miles long, and each family member was allotted an adjacent strip of land.

Castillo County, the San Luis Valley and most of the Southwest were originally part of Mexico, and the Borregos were one of hundreds of pre–Colorado Territory settlers granted land by the government of Mexico. The irrigation system that they built, known as the San Luis Peoples' Ditch, was no different than prehistoric channels and water basins built in arid lands by the first people to settle at Mesa Verde in AD 550.

Going back several millennia, one requirement in human settlements was and is common: a year-round water supply was needed for survival. Whether it was water for drinking or for growing crops to feed families, redirecting streamflows to sustain the community was a necessity.

Feliz's recorded family ties to the Southwest date back to the late 1700s and northern New Mexico, where his father, Nicholas Antonio Borrego, resided in the San Juan Pueblo twenty-five miles north of Santa Fe. The pueblo was founded around the year 1200, but Spanish conquistador Don Juan de Oñate took control of the pueblo in 1598 and established the first Spanish capital of New Mexico nearby.

Castillo County was the first area of Colorado to have permanent settlements. Hispanic settlers from Taos, New Mexico, established San Luis in 1851. In 1852, Feliz and several other men from the San Luis homesteads traveled east, probably to Kansas, where the government for Kansas Territory was being established, to register the water right for the Peoples' Ditch, the oldest irrigation system in Colorado in continuous use. The Peoples' Ditch is the earliest recognized water right in the state.

After the Mexican-American War, Castillo County and the San Luis Valley were declared part of the Kansas Territory in 1854, then the Colorado Territory in 1861. Mexican land grant families were promised their farmland in perpetuity under the Treaty of Guadalupe Hidalgo, but Mexican Americans lost 80 percent of original land grants via high property taxes imposed on Mexican American landowners, in some cases five times higher than those paid by White neighbors.

The Borregos persevered and eventually relocated to three hundred acres of land along Trujillo Creek (Apishapa Creek), east of Aguilar, Colorado, in the late 1800s. Around 1880, Feliz de Jesus Borrego and his son Juan Luis both filed General Land Office homestead patents for their land near the Comanche National Grasslands. The area around Aguilar mirrored Lafayette, in that farmers could earn wages by working in Southern Coal Field mines during peak demand in the winter months.

The Borrego family's pioneering and farming legacy passed to Feliz's grandson Joseph Garfield Borrego, who left Las Animas County in 1911 with his wife, Emiliana, and established a new generation of farming along Coal Creek east of Lafayette in 1912.

THE SPANISH "RIGHT OF thirst" water rights system, which recognizes community water rights, was used by Colorado's first acequias in southern Colorado. In 1879, Colorado adopted the Prior Appropriation Doctrine, which codified the "first-in-time, first-in-right" principal of water allocation.

Water rights were allocated by the date a diversion ditch was constructed, a priority system first adopted by gold miners during the late 1850s California gold rush. Irrigation ditches along year-round water courses fed by Colorado's high-mountain snowfall were cherished. Diverted streamflows from Boulder Creek, South Boulder Creek, St. Vrain Creek, Big Thompson River and Cache la Poudre River allowed Colorado's northern Front Range agricultural industry to prosper.

Some of the first recorded irrigation ditches in Boulder County were noted by General Land Office surveyors in the early 1860s. White settlers along Boulder Creek north of Lafayette constructed several diversion structures, as did farmers south of Louisville, who redirected water from Coal Creek starting in the late 1850s.

As the years progressed since those first local irrigation systems, Lafayette's dominant industries—coal mining, brick making, flour milling, passenger trains and steam-powered electrical generation—have disappeared, but the infrastructure for irrigating life-sustaining crops, and the rights associated with the water supply, remains today.

THE PRIMARY DITCH SERVING early Lafayette farmers, the Goodhue Ditch, was completed by Abner C. Goodhue in about 1875. Goodhue built a diversion structure on South Boulder Creek to service his farm along Rock Creek near today's Dillon Road.

As early as 1860, farmers including Adolf Waneka avoided using Rock Creek and Coal Creek for irrigation purposes. Year-round streamflows in Coal Creek and Rock Creek, which originates above Golden Gate Canyon State Park in Gilpin County, are low except for in spring, when foothills' snowmelt and rainstorms increase the streamflow. Farmers near Marshall obtained early rights to the stream's meager supply, leaving little for downstream users. This meant that Joe Borrego, whose farm was located just south of today's Erie Air Park, couldn't depend on Coal Creek for crops, but the family did raise livestock, including cows, sheep, pigs and chickens.

Goodhue Ditch shareholder Mary Miller and her son George irrigated the Miller Farm in south Lafayette via the north branch of the Goodhue Ditch that runs near the Lafayette Cemetery. The Miller feeder ditch paralleled Public Road before emptying into Miller Reservoir at today's South Public Road and South Boulder Road. Mary Miller and the Harmon family held ownership in Henry Waneka Reservoir No. 2, known today as Waneka Lake, which Lafayette purchased for water storage in the 1970s.

Prior to 1900, Lafayette residents relied on backyard water wells for drinking water. Only after the 1901 fire on East Simpson Street that destroyed fifteen buildings did the town board consider acquiring and storing water to be used in downtown fire hydrants. A deep well on the east edge of town was considered, but the board chose to acquire Davidson Ditch and Dry Creek Ditch water rights, and water from the 1870s-era irrigation ditches was used to fill two reservoirs. Like the Goodhue Ditch, the Davidson and Dry Creek were sourced from South Boulder Creek.

Lafayette's primitive water distribution system had its faults, namely an inadequate filtration system at the two town reservoirs near today's Baseline Road and U.S. 287. Volunteer firefighters often encountered fish plugging the hydrants, and there was no infrastructure to purify the water for consumption. Citizens who did tap into the town water supply were advised to boil drinking water, and in summer months wood barrels with drinking water were dispersed along East Simpson Street. In 1906, the editor of the *Lafayette News Free Press* opined that "under these conditions there is a grain of truth in the annual joke, that bad water is largely responsible for excessive beer drinking."

Proposals to store water in the abandoned coal mines under Lafayette surfaced throughout Lafayette's history. The Simpson Mine was known by local miners as a "wet" mine. Sump pumps worked twenty-four hours a day to clear the water seepage from the haulageways and shafts. Abandoned in 1926, the mine filled with water, and farmer Charles "Chuck" Waneka purchased the rights from the property owner in the 1950s to pump water out of the Simpson Mine, about 250 feet underground. In 1997, Waneka was forced to abandon the pump after the state water court denied Waneka's request for an adjudicated (legally decreed) well. The pump is still intact and operable.

In 1909, the town built a 150,000-gallon storage tank a block west of Public Road on Geneseo Street and updated the wood supply lines coming from the town reservoirs. At a cost of $125,000, a twenty-inch steel pipeline was built from the reservoirs to Old Town. Mayor Thomas Beynon pushed the town board to approve a diversion structure at Eldorado Springs so that South Boulder Creek water could flow directly to Lafayette reservoirs (instead of through the various ditches). Town employees incorporated a sand bed filtration system into the diversion structure. In the 1920s, the town moved the Eldorado Springs diversion structure upstream from Eldorado Springs, because those residents were dumping raw sewage into South Boulder Creek. In 1936, at a cost of $15,000, a modern water filtration plant was built along Baseline Road west of the two Lafayette reservoirs. A town-wide sewage treatment facility for Lafayette wasn't completed until 1948.

The 1990s was a pivotal decade for water used in irrigation. As housing growth in Colorado Front Range cities exploded, shares in water conveyed by irrigation ditches for growing crops became scarcer and more expensive. Water in the Colorado Big Thompson (CBT) water project hovered at $2,000 per share in 1980 and reached $15,000 per share in 2000. In 2020, a share of CBT was selling for $63,000.

Water once dedicated to family farms is now flowing from faucets and showers in new homes in Lafayette. But satisfying the thirst for a growing city has been a decades-old pursuit for Lafayette city staff and planners. As a result, Lafayette is in a better position to make it through drought years and can sustain continued growth.

Lafayette's water sources include South Boulder Creek, Boulder Creek and Coal Creek, which is stored in Baseline, Waneka and Goose Haven reservoirs. Lafayette has a share of interest in the Coal Ridge, Davidson, Dry Creek 2, Dry Creek Carrier, Enterprise, Goodhue, Leyner-Cottonwood, Lower Boulder and South Boulder & Bear Creek irrigation ditches.

Recent additions to the city's water portfolio include CBT project shares for water stored in Boulder Reservoir, Carter Lake, Lake Granby, Horsetooth Reservoir and Shadow Mountain Reservoir. Lafayette's inclusion in the Northern Colorado Water Conservancy District will bring water from new reservoirs northwest of Fort Collins to Lafayette, Fort Morgan, Erie, Dacono, Eaton and several other Front Range communities.

The San Luis Peoples' Ditch, a legacy to Feliz de Jesus Borrego and early Latino farmers in southern Colorado, still serves sixteen "paricantes," or members, and irrigates more than two thousand acres of hay and crops.

BIBLIOGRAPHY

Introduction

Hall, J. Knox, ed. *Stark County, Illinois and Its People: A Record of Settlement, Organization, Progress and Achievement.* Chicago: Pioneer Publishing, 1916.

Lafayette College. "Soldier. Scholar. Revolutionary. Hero of Two Worlds." 2020. https://about.lafayette.edu.

Leeson, M.A. *Documents and Biography Pertaining to the Settlement and Progress of Stark County, Illinois: Containing an authentic summary of records, documents, historical works and newspapers relating to Indian history, original settlement, organization and politics, courts and bar, citizen soldiers, military societies, marriages, churches, schools, secret, benevolent and literary societies, etc.: together with biography of representative men of the past and present.* Chicago: M.A. Leeson & Company, 1887.

McNamara, Robert. "Visit of Marquis de Lafayette to All 24 States." ThoughtCo.com. Updated May 22, 2019. https://www.thoughtco.com.

Shallenberger, E.H. *Stark County and Its Pioneers.* Cambridge, IL: B.W. Seaton, Prairie Chief Office, 1989.

1. A Peoples Erased

Boulder (CO) Daily Camera, November 15, 2014.

Burney, Michael S., and Barbara L. Scott. "The Past Supercedes the Future, for the Present, at Valmont Butte." *Applied Anthropologist* (2006).

Coel, Margaret. *Chief Left Hand.* Norman: University of Oklahoma Press, 1981.

Coffin, Morse H. "The Battle at Sand Creek." From series of articles in the *Colorado Sun*, 1879.

Crossen, Forest. "Anthony Arnett—Empire Builder." *Colorado Magazine* (September 1946).

Dyni, Anne. *Pioneer Voices of the Boulder Valley*. Boulder, CO: Boulder County Parks and Open Space Department, 1989.

Fridtjof, David, and Andrew E. Masich. *Halfbreed: The Remarkable True Story of George Bent*. Cambridge, MA: Da Capo Press, 2004.

Gardner, A. Dudley. *Historic Assessment of the Cherokee Trail and Bryan to Brown's Park Road Within the Wold Trona Lease Area*. Rock Springs: Western Wyoming Community College, 1994.

Gladden, Sanford Charles. "Early Days of Boulder, Colorado," Boulder Carnegie Library for Local History Collection, 1982.

Gleichman, Peter J., Carol L. Gleichman and Sarah L. Karhu. *Excavations at the Rock Creek Site: 1990–1993*. Denver: Colorado Historical Society, 1993.

Grinnell, George Bird. *The Fighting Cheyennes*. New York: Charles Scribner's Sons, 1915.

Hafen, LeRoy R. "Cherokee Goldseekers in Colorado, 1849–1850." *Colorado Magazine* (May 1938).

Howbert, Irving. *Indians of the Pike's Peak Region*. Aurora, CO: Bibliographical Center for Research, 1914.

Hyde, George E. *Life of George Bent*. Norman: University of Oklahoma Press, 1968.

Isaac, Margaret. "Childhood Memories of Kittie Hall Fairfield." *Colorado Magazine* (October 1959).

Ives, Ronald L. "Early Human Occupation of the Colorado Headwaters Region: An Archeological Reconnaissance." *Geographical Review* 32, no. 3 (July 1942): 448–62.

Marshall, S.L.A. *Crimsoned Prairie: The Indian Wars*. New York: Hachette Books, 1972.

McDermott, John D. *Circle of Fire: The Indian War of 1865*. Mechanicsburg, PA: Stackpole Books, 2003.

McGrath, Maria Davies. *The Real Pioneers of Colorado*. Denver, CO: Denver Museum, 1934.

Stewart, Jennie E. "Beginnings at Boulder, Red Rock: First White Camp in Boulder County." Boulder, CO: Boulder Carnegie Library for Local History, 1929.

Urquhart, Lena M. *Colorow: The Angry Chief*. Denver, CO: Golden Bell Press. 1968.

Waneka, Charles "Chuck." Personal interview. 2015.

West, Elliot. *The Contested Plains: Indians, Goldseekers, and the Rush to Colorado*. Lawrence: University Press of Kansas, 1998.

2. Cultivating the Wide-Open Spaces

Boulder County Clerk and Recorder. Digitized deeds and property records. Boulder County, Colorado.

Bureau of Land Management/General Land Office. Digitized land patent records. Washington, D.C.

Grinnell, George Bird. *The Fighting Cheyennes*. New York: Charles Scribner's Sons, 1915.

History of Clear Creek and Boulder Valleys, Colorado. Chicago, IL: O.L. Baskin & Company, 1880.

Hofstadter, Richard. *The Age of Reform: From Bryan to FDR*. Alfred A Knopf, 1955;

Hyde, George E. *Life of George Bent*. Norman: University of Oklahoma Press, 1968.

Lafayette Historical Society. *Lafayette, Colorado History: Treeless Plain to Thriving City*. Raleigh, NC: Curtis Media, 1990.

Stewart, Jennie. A. "Boulder County Pioneers." Prepared for the Arapahoe Chapter of the Daughters of the American Revolution. Boulder County, Colorado, 1946–48.

Stone, Wilbur Fiske. "William Waneka" (profile). *History of Colorado*. Vol. 4. Chicago, IL: S.J. Clarke Publishing, 1919.

Zabriskie, James C. "Public Lands: "General Laws of Congress in Relation to the Public Lands of the United States." Washington, D.C.: U.S. Bureau of Land Management, 1870.

3. A Town Takes Shape

Alamosa Journal. May 8, 1884.

Boulder County Clerk and Recorder. Digitized deeds and property records. Boulder County, Colorado.

Boulder District Court records at the Colorado State Archives. Denver, Colorado.

Carson, Dina. "Boulder County Commissioners Journal No. 1, 1861–1871." 2016.

"Early Days in Boulder County." *The Trail: A Magazine for Colorado* (February 1911).

"History of Church Ranch and the Church Family." City of Westminster, 2010.

History of Clear Creek and Boulder Valleys, Colorado. Chicago, IL: O.L. Baskin & Company, 1880.

Hutchison, James D. *Survey and Settlement—Lafayette, Colorado.* Lafayette, CO: Morrell Graphics, 1994.

Lafayette Leader, February 14, 1908; October 16, 1911; March 8, 1905; May 10, 1957.

Lafayette News, March 15, 1902.

Lafayette News Free Press, April 14, 1906.

Lafayette Public Library oral history transcript featuring Frank Miller. Lafayette, Colorado.

"Personal Interview by Bancroft, J.B. Foote, Boulder, Colorado, 1886." Lafayette Public Library. Lafayette, Colorado.

Spitler, Laura L., and Lou Walther. *Gem of The Mountain Valley: A History of Broomfield.* Broomfield, CO: Broomfield Centennial-Bicentennial Commission, 1975.

West, Elliot. *The Saloon on the Rocky Mountain Mining Frontier.* Lincoln: University of Nebraska Press, 1979.

Westover, Karen. "Mary Elizabeth Foote Miller." Lafayette Public Library. Lafayette, Colorado, 2012.

Wilber, Mary. Personal interviews with the great-granddaughter of John Franklin Miller, 2015 and 2016.

Wolfenbarger, Deon. "Boulder County's Agricultural Heritage." Boulder, CO: Boulder County Parks and Open Space Department, 2006.

4. A Town Built on Coal Mining

Bell, William Abraham. *New Tracks in North America.* London: Chapman and Hall, 1869.

Boulder County Clerk and Recorder. Digitized deeds and property records. Boulder, Colorado.

Bureau of Land Management/General Land Office. Field notes of General Land Office surveyor Hiram Witter, 1864.

Coal Age, March 14, 1914.

Colorado Division of Reclamation, Mining and Safety. Lafayette coal history. Denver, Colorado.

Conarroe, Carolyn J. *The Louisville Story*. N.p.: Conarroe, 1978.

Denver Daily News, January 21, 1898.

"Early Discoveries of Coal in America." *Coal and Coke Operator and the Fuel Magazine of Pittsburgh and Chicago* (1913).

"An Early Pennsylvania Coal Discovery." *Coal Trade Journal* (January 1900).

1899–1900 Biennial Report of the Colorado Inspector of Coal Mines. State of Colorado.

Lafayette Historical Society. *Lafayette, Colorado History: Treeless Plain to Thriving City*. Raleigh, NC: Curtis Media, 1990.

Lafayette Public Library oral history tape collection, including Jack Davies, Bob Johnson, Lawrence Amicarella and Sam Marino. Lafayette, Colorado.

Martin, Richard. *Coal Wars*. New York: St. Martin's Press, 2015.

Munroe, Charles E. "Bulletin 17: The Primer on Explosives for Coal Miners." Department of Interior, Bureau of Mines, 1911.

Norman, Kathleen. "1999 Architectural Survey of Old Town Lafayette." City of Lafayette, Colorado, 1989.

"Report on the Operations of the Coal-Testing Plant of the U.S. Geological Survey." Washington, D.C.: U.S. Geological Survey, 1906.

Smith, Phyllis. *Once a Coal Miner: The Story of Colorado's Northern Coal Field*. Boulder, CO: Pruett Publishing Company, 1989.

Stone, Wilbur Fiske. "C.C. Welch" (profile). *History of Colorado*. Vol. 4. Chicago: S.J. Clarke Publishing, 1919.

The Travelers Insurance Company. "Hazards of Coal Mining." 1916.

United States Department of Energy. "A Brief History of Coal Use." Washington, D.C. 2015.

Whiteside, James. *Regulating Danger: The Struggle for Mine Safety in the Rocky Mountain Coal Industry*. Lincoln: University of Nebraska Press, 1990.

5. *The Liquor Clause*

Boulder District Court records at the Colorado State Archives. Denver, Colorado.

Carson, Dina. "Boulder County Commissioners Journal No. 1, 1861–1871." Niwot, CO: Iron Gate Publishing, 2013.

Daily Camera, October 1891.

"Early Days in Boulder County." *The Trail: A Magazine for Colorado* (February 1911).

Harper, Jane C. *Colorado Newspapers: A History & Inventory, 1859–2000*. Denver, CO: Colorado Press Association, 2014.

History of Clear Creek and Boulder Valleys, Colorado. Chicago, IL: O.L. Baskin & Company, 1880.

Kolar, Dorothy. Facts on Early Lafayette (column). *Lafayette Leader*, 1952–57.

Lafayette Leader, February 14, 1908; October 16, 1911; March 8, 1905; January 12, 1934; May 10, 1957.

Lafayette News, March 15, 1902.

Lafayette News Free Press, April 14, 1906.

Lafayette Public Library oral history transcript featuring Frank Miller. Lafayette, Colorado.

6. Notable Places Lost and Found

Aspen Daily Times, June 24, 1904.

"Colorado Architects Biographical Sketch." Denver: Colorado Historical Society, 2002.

Cramer, Anne. "Reference List of Buildings in Lafayette, Colorado." Updated and kept current by the Lafayette Historical Society, 1980.

Daily Camera, February 3, February 13 and August 1, 1896; June 18, 1986; September 1, 1892.

Gaz, Louis. Personal interview, 2015.

Hutchison, Jim. *Survey and Settlement—Lafayette, Colorado*. Lafayette, CO: Morrell Graphics, 1994.

Lafayette Historical Society. *Lafayette, Colorado History: Treeless Plain to Thriving City*. Raleigh, NC: Curtis Media, 1990.

Lafayette Leader, May 11, September 7, 1917; May 3, May 11, June 21, June 28, July 5, July 12, August 16, August 30, October 18, November 30, 1918; February 27, 1964.

Lafayette News, November 20, 1975; October 2, 1985, June 18, 1986.

Miller, Frank. School presentations from oral history transcripts at the Lafayette Public Library. Lafayette, Colorado, 1964 and 1968.

Norman, Cathleen. "Lafayette 2008 Commercial and Agricultural Properties Survey." City of Lafayette, Colorado, 2008.

Rocky Mountain Fuel Company records. Denver Public Library, Western History Collection.

Salida Mail, January 31, 1890.

7. Ancient Trails and Steel Rails

Babal, Marianne. Personal correspondence with Senior Historian, Wells Fargo Historical Services, 2017.

Boulder County Clerk and Recorder. Boulder County, Colorado.

Burke, Marril Lee. *A Bumpy Ride: History of Stagecoaching in Colorado*. Lake City, CO: Western Reflections Publishing, 2007.

Colorado Division of Reclamation, Mining and Safety. Denver, Colorado.

Conarroe, Carolyn. *Coal Mining in Colorado's Northern Field*. N.p.: Conarroe, 2001.

Daily Camera, August 10, 1895.

Denver Daily Tribune, March 31, 1878.

Estes Park Trail Gazette, January 8, 1926.

Fort Collins Courier, May 24, 1913.

Frazier, Jimmie Lee. "Early Stage Lines in Colorado, 1859–1865." Thesis, University of Denver, 1959.

Frederick, J.V. *Ben Holladay: The Stagecoach King*. Lincoln: University of Nebraska Press. 1968

Lafayette Historical Society. *Lafayette, Colorado History: Treeless Plain to Thriving City*. Raleigh, NC: Curtis Media, 1990.

Lafayette Leader. January 15, 1926.

Longmont Daily Times, January 23, March 3, June 11, July 10 and July 17, 1926; January 18, 1927.

Louisville Times interview of Lew Wilson, 1950.

Noel, Thomas and Dan Corson. *Boulder County: An Illustrated History*. New York: Heritage Press, 1999.

"Portrait and Biographical Record of Denver and Vicinity, Colorado," Chapman Publishing Co., 1898.

"Report on the Development of the Mineral and other Resources of Colorado," by J. Alden Smith, 1883

Rocky Mountain News, February 27, 1869.

Sampson, Joanna. *Walking Through History on Marshall Mesa*. Boulder, CO: City of Boulder Open Space and Mountain Parks, 1995.

Smiley, Jerome C. *History of Denver*. Denver, CO: The Denver Times, The Times-Sun Publishing, 1901.

State of Colorado. Office of the Railroad Commission. "First Annual Report of the Railroad Commissioner of the State of Colorado for Year Ending June 30, 1885." Denver, CO: Collier & Cleaveland Lithograph Company, 1886.

Waneka, Charles "Chuck" Personal interview. 2015.

8. A Union Town

Aldrich, Mark. "History of Workplace Safety in the United States, 1880–1970." Northampton, MA: Smith College, 2015.

Black Diamond, November 22, 1913.

Boulder County News, April 20, 1877.

Chaffee County Republic, February 17, 1898.

Chintz, B.M. "Explosions in Colorado Coal Mines, 1883 to 1932." Washington, D.C.: U.S. Bureau of Mines, 1933.

Conarroe, Carolyn. *Coal Mining in Colorado's Northern Field*. N.p.: Conarroe, 2001.

Daily Camera, February 1, 1893.

Denver Advocate, August 19, 1898.

Denver Daily News, February 3, 1898.

Ed Doyle papers. Denver Public Library, Western History Collection, WH 126.

Hofstadter, Richard. *The Age of Reform: From Bryan to FDR*. New York: Vintage, 1955.

Hutchison, Jim. *Survey and Settlement—Lafayette, Colorado*. Lafayette, CO: Morrell Graphics, 1994.

James Cannon Jr. and Mary (Lowman) Cannon scrapbook. Denver Public Library, Western History Collection, 1897–98.

Kellett, Bill. Author's conversations, 1997–2000.

Lafayette Historical Society. *Lafayette, Colorado History: Treeless Plain to Thriving City*. Raleigh, NC: Curtis Media, 1990.

Lafayette Leader, October 20, 1922.

Lafayette Public Library. Oral history transcript collection featuring Joe "Cotton" Fletcher, Henry "Welchie" Mathias and Chelmar "Shine" Miller.

Louisville Historian (Spring 2012). Louisville Historical Society, 2012.

Martin, Richard. *Coal Wars*. New York: St. Martin's Press, 2015.

McMahon, Ronald Lorren. "Visual Sociology: A Study of the Western Coal Miner." PhD dissertation, University of Colorado, 1975.

Muncy, Robyn. *Relentless Reformer: Josephine Roche and Progressivism*. Princeton, NJ: Princeton University Press. 2013;

"Official Labor Directory and Manual of the Colorado State Federation of Labor." Denver, Colorado. 1907.

Official Meeting Minutes of the UMWA Local 1388. Lafayette Public Library collection. Lafayette, Colorado.

Rocky Mountain Fuel Company collection at the Denver Public Library, Western History Collection.

Rocky Mountain News, August 2, 1898.

Sinclair, Upton. *The Coal War*. Boulder: University Press of Colorado, 1976.

Smith, Phyllis. *Once a Coal Miner: The Story of Colorado's Northern Coal Field*. Boulder, CO: Pruett Publishing, 1989

Somerhousen, Marc. *The Working Rules in the Bituminous Mining Industry*. Madison: University of Wisconsin–Madison, 1922.

State of Colorado. "1901–1902 Colorado Department of Labor Biennial Report." Denver, Colorado.

United Mine Workers Journal, 1915 and 1916.

United States Congress. "Final Report and Testimony Submitted to the U.S. Congress from the Commission on Industrial Relations." 1916.

United States Department of Interior, Bureau of Mines. "Hazards of Mining: Coal-Mine Fatalities in the United States, 1870–1914." 1916.

United States Senate. "A Report to the U.S. Senate on Labor Disturbances in the State of Colorado from 1880 to 1904." 1905.

Van Kleeck, Mary. "Miners and Management: A Study of the Collective Agreement between the United Mine Workers of America and the Rocky Mountain Fuel Company." New York: Russell Sage Foundation, 1934.

Whiteside, James. *Regulating Danger: The Struggle for Mine Safety in the Rocky Mountain Coal Industry*. Lincoln: University of Nebraska Press, 1990.

9. *Breaking the Barrier*

Employers Mutual Insurance Company records. Rocky Mountain Fuel Company Collection at the University of Colorado.

Lafayette Leader, June 22, 1917; October 11, 1918.

Oral history tape recording of Louis "Bigshoe" Brugger. Colorado Coal Project. University of Colorado Archives.

Owens, Lupie O., and Richard Hill's narratives in Lafayette Historical Society. *Lafayette, Colorado History: Treeless Plain to Thriving City*. Raleigh, NC: Curtis Media, 1990.

Rees, Michael J. "Chicanos Mine the Columbine: An Hispanic Workforce In Northern Colorado." Department of History, University of Colorado, 1995.

Rocky Mountain Fuel Company Map Collection. Lafayette Public Library. Lafayette, Colorado.

State of Colorado. "12th Annual Colorado Coal Mine Inspector's Report." 1924.

UMWA Lafayette Local 1388 meeting minutes, 1903–32. Lafayette Public Library. Lafayette, Colorado.

United States Federal Census, 1910, 1920 and 1930.

10. Remnants of Industry

Armstrong, Gerald R. "Jerry." Personal interviews, 2015.

Boulder County Clerk and Recorder. Boulder, Colorado.

Campbell, Elizabeth. "Abstract of the Rocky Mountain Fuel Company Collection." University of Colorado–Boulder Libraries.

Colorado Republican, May 17, 1906.

Colorado Trade Journal, 1897.

Conarroe, Carolyn. *Coal Mining in Colorado's Northern Field*. N.p.: Conarroe, 2001.

Corbett & Ballenger's Annual Denver City Directory. 1891–99.

Denver Post, November 24, 1952.

Denver Times, May 25, 1898.

Fredell, Helen. "Letters of Edgar Edmund (E.E.) Shumway, 1862–1914," and Rocky Mountain Fuel Company history from the Shumway Family, edited by great-granddaughter of Herbert Shumway, E.E. Shumway's brother.

Gladden, Sanford. *Early Days of Boulder*, Vol. 1. Boulder, CO: Boulder Genealogical Society, 1982.

James Cannon Jr. and Mary (Lowman) Cannon scrapbook. Denver Public Library, Western History Collection, 1897–98.

Lafayette Historical Society. *Lafayette, Colorado History: Treeless Plain to Thriving City*. Raleigh, NC: Curtis Media, 1990.

Lafayette Leader, April 13, April 27, May 4 and September 28, 1905; May 3 and May 17, 1906; May 1940.

Lafayette News, September 7 and September 21, 1905.

McGinn, Elinor. *A Wide-Awake Woman: Josephine Roche in the Era of Reform*. Denver: Colorado Historical Society. 2003.

Moody's Analysis of Investments, 1921.

Muncy, Robyn. *Relentless Reformer: Josephine Roche and Progressivism*. Princeton, NJ: Princeton University Press, 2015.

Oak Creek Times, October 12, 1911.

Omaha Daily Bee, October 4, 1903.

Patten, Andrew. *History of Waneka Lake*. Lafayette, Colorado, 2006.

"Providing Energy for More than a Century." Public Service Company of Colorado, 1976.

Redmond, Anji. "Lafayette Historic Preservation Board application for City of Lafayette Historic Landmark." 2015. Rocky Mountain Fuel Company corporate records at the Denver Public Library, Western History Collection, WH963.

Rocky Mountain News, January 12, 1914; January 14 and February 7, 1927; April 20, 1975.

Rocky Mountain Stores Company: Rocky Mountain Fuel Company Collection. Denver Public Library, Western History Collection.

Van Kleek, Mary. "Miners and Management: A Study of the Collective Agreement between the United Mine Workers of America and the Rocky Mountain Fuel Company." New York: Russell Sage Foundation, 1934.

Waneka, Charles "Chuck." Personal interviews, 2015 and 2016.

11. A Dark Period Comes to Light

Archuleta, Frank. Personal interviews, 2019–21.

Burek, Josh. "What Are the Origins of Cross-Burning?" *Christian Science Monitor*, December 13, 2002.

City of Lafayette. "Latino Legacy in Lafayette: A History of Civil Rights Struggle." Lafayette, CO: City of Lafayette, 2019.

Colorado Supreme Court. *Lueras v. Town of Lafayette, case 9509, 1934*. Colorado State Archives.

Dunn, Meg. "Colorado Women of the Ku Klux Klan, Part 5." NorthernColoradoHistory.com, 2019.

Lafayette Historical Society. *Lafayette, Colorado History: Treeless Plain to Thriving City*. Raleigh, NC: Curtis Media, 1990.

Lafayette Leader, 1916–35.

Louisville Times, March 17, 1993.

Lund, Claudia. "The Uninvited: History of the KKK in Lafayette." Lafayette Miners Museum newsletter, Fall 2015.

McIntosh, Marjorie K. *Latinos of Boulder County, Colorado, 1900–1980*. Palm Springs, CA: Old John Publishing, 2016.

Oral history interviews featuring Boughton Noble, Lawrence Amicarella and Sally Martinez from the Boulder Carnegie Library for Local History.

Quillen, Ed. "Welcome to Kolorado, Klan Kountry." *Colorado Springs Independent*, May 22, 2003.

Rocky Mountain American, January 1923–July 1923.

State of Colorado. Clarence C. Morley Collection at the Colorado State Archives.

United States Federal Census, 1910, 1920 and 1930.

Zick, Timothy. "Cross Burning, Cockfighting, and Symbolic Meaning: Toward a First Amendment Ethnography." *William & Mary Law Review* 45, no. 5 (2004).

12. Sustaining a Community

Borrego, Robert, and Bill Kellett. "Narratives Printed in Lafayette Historical Society." *Lafayette, Colorado History: Treeless Plain to Thriving City*. Raleigh, NC: Curtis Media, 1990.

Colorado State University, Colorado Water Center. "Colorado Water Knowledge: Water History." 2020.

Delgado, Richard, and Jean Stefancic. "Home Grown Racism: Colorado's Historic Embrace—and Denial—of Equal Opportunity in Higher Education." *University of Colorado Law Review* 703 (1999).

Goudy, Frank. *Semi-Centennial History of the State of Colorado*. Vol. 1. Chicago, IL: Lewis Publishing Company, 1913.

Lafayette News Free-Press, December 4, 1908; December 11, 1936.

Muniz, Gloria Jean (Ruybal). "Borrego-Muniz: Ancestors & Descendants of Garfield E. Muniz, 1745–2013." N.p., 2013.

Orr, John. "Coyote Gulch: A Look at the San Luis People's Ditch." Coyote Gulch. May 2, 2010. Accessed 2020. https://coyotegulch.blog.

Sangre de Cristo Acequia Association. Colorado Acequia Handbook. 2016.

Short, Douglas. "City of Lafayette Water Conservation Plan." Lafayette, CO: City of Lafayette, 2010.

United States National Parks Service. "San Luis People's Ditch" HAER No. CO-96. 1996.

INDEX

ABOUT THE AUTHOR

Doug Conarroe is a fourth-generation Coloradan who grew up in Louisville, Colorado. He and his wife, Dana Coffield, moved to Lafayette, Colorado, in 1995.

Besides having a passion for local history, Doug is an avid recycler of neglected and abandoned historic homes, taking them from uninhabitable structures to modern, family-friendly homes.

Doug has served on the Lafayette Historic Preservation Board and is a past president and board member of Historic Boulder. He joined the Lafayette Historical Society as a lifetime member in about 1998.

He has a journalism degree and an MBA from the University of Colorado and worked for the family newspaper before joining the *Denver Post* and then the *(Tacoma) News Tribune*. He published the *North Forty News* from 2011 to 2017.